FIELDHOUSE

WRITTEN BY
SCOTT NOVOSEL

DRAWN BY
SAM SHARPE

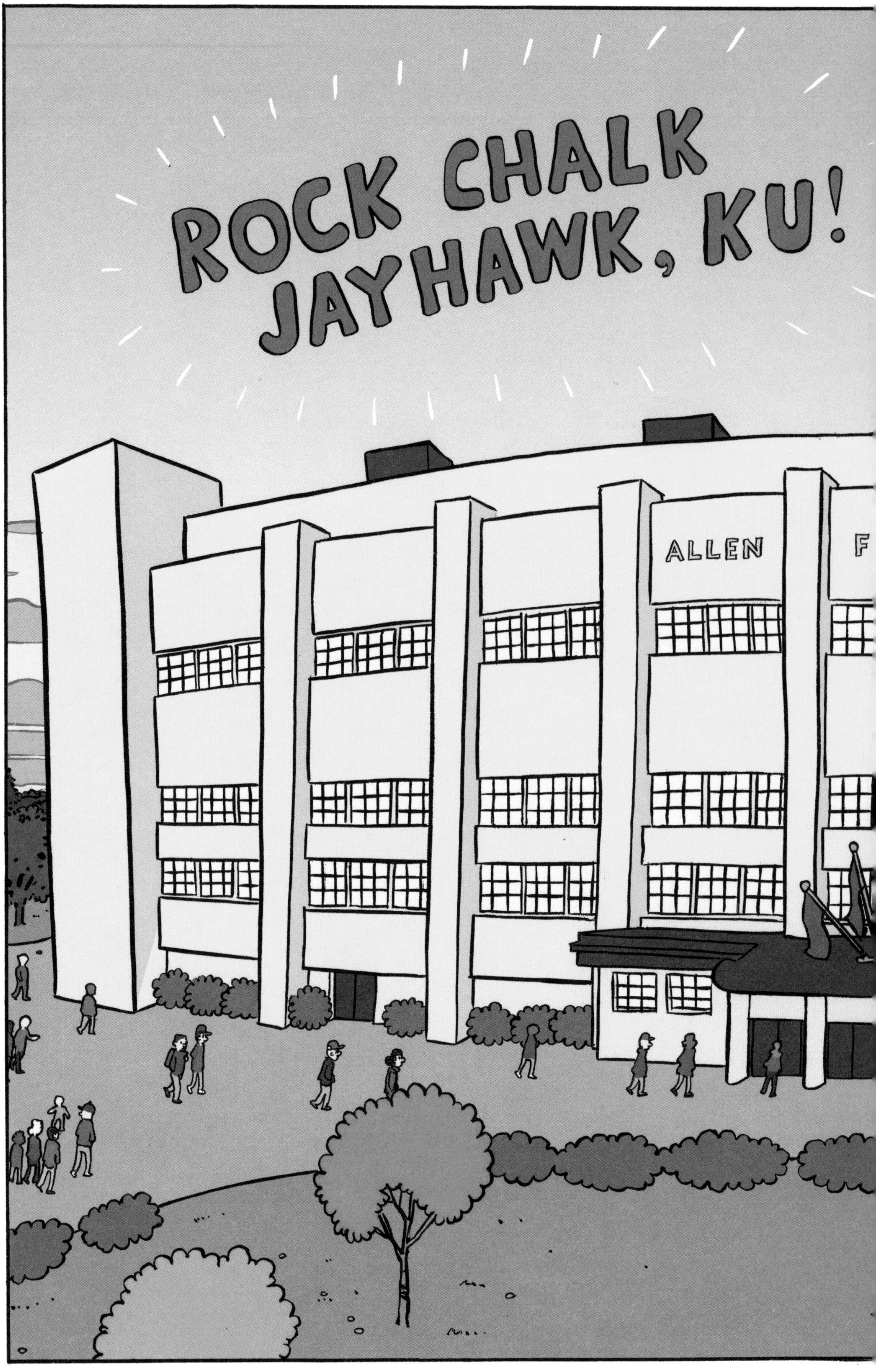
ROCK CHALK
JAYHAWK, KU!
ALLEN F

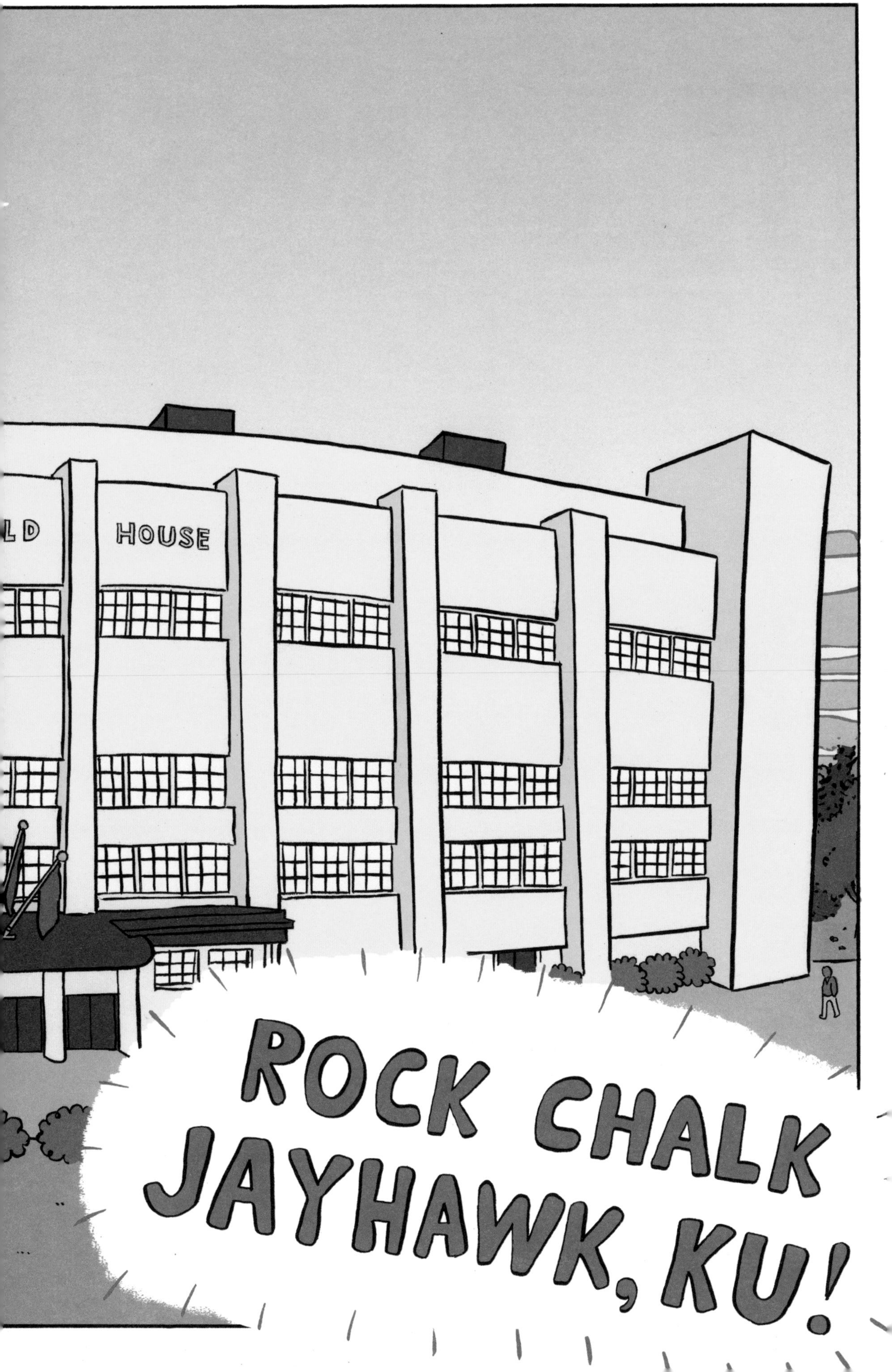
LD HOUSE
ROCK CHALK JAYHAWK, KU!

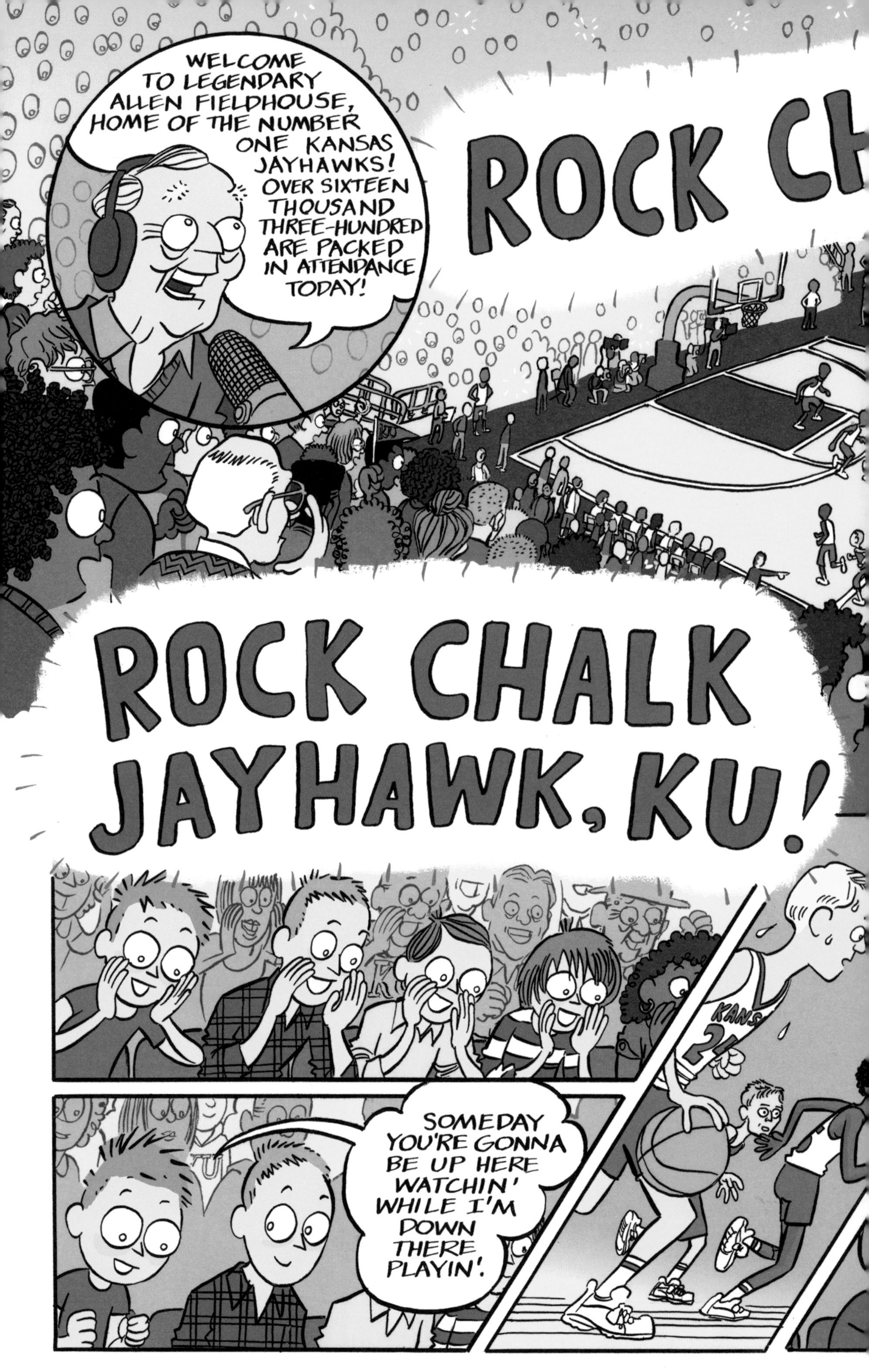
WELCOME TO LEGENDARY ALLEN FIELDHOUSE, HOME OF THE NUMBER ONE KANSAS JAYHAWKS! OVER SIXTEEN THOUSAND THREE-HUNDRED ARE PACKED IN ATTENDANCE TODAY!
ROCK CH
ROCK CHALK JAYHAWK, KU!
KANS
SOMEDAY YOU'RE GONNA BE UP HERE WATCHIN' WHILE I'M DOWN THERE PLAYIN'.

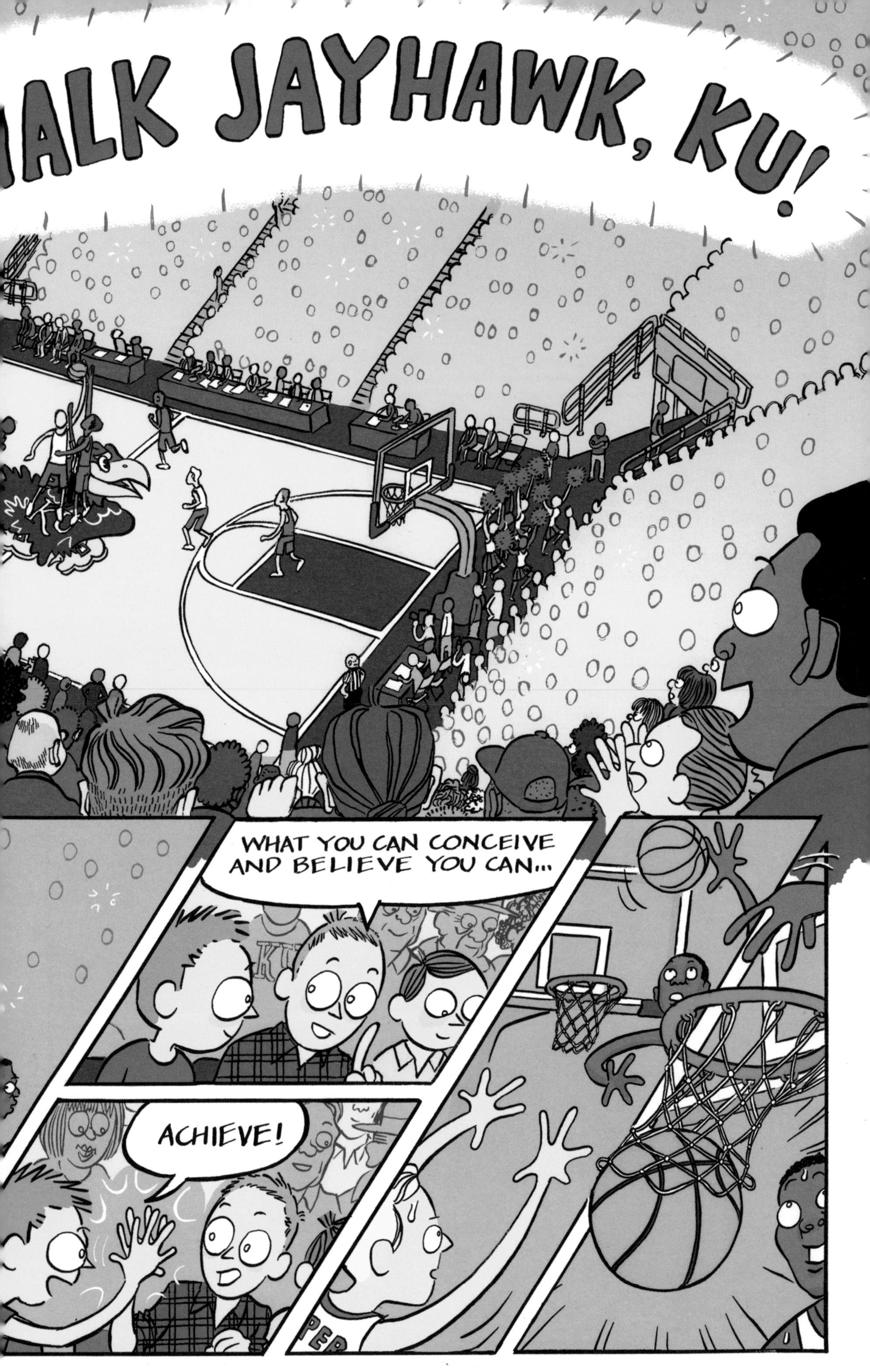
ALK JAYHAWK, KU!
WHAT YOU CAN CONCEIVE AND BELIEVE YOU CAN...
ACHIEVE!

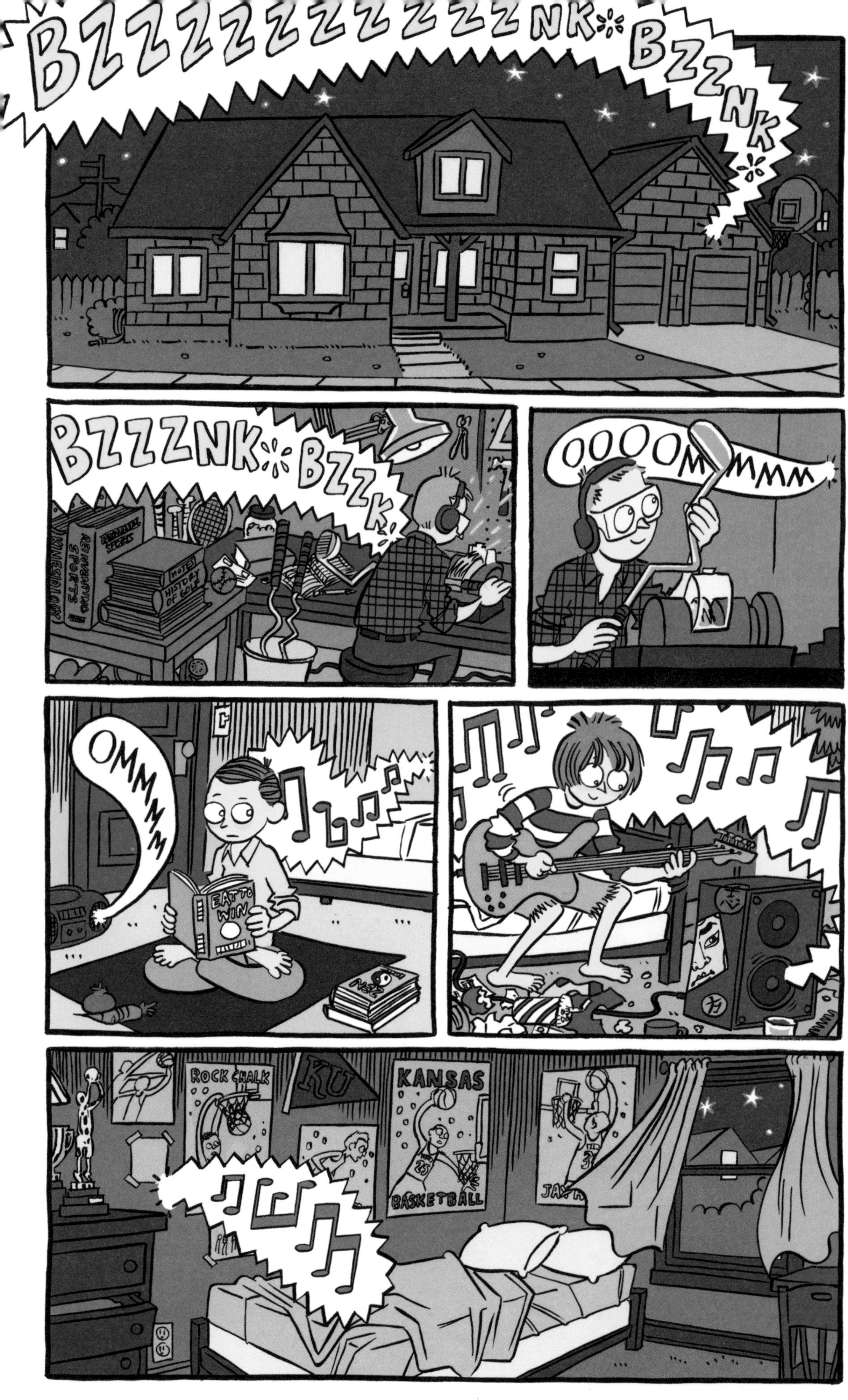

BZZZZZZZZZZNK
BZZNK
BZZZZNK
BZZZK
KINESIOLOGY
REINVIGORATING SPORTS
NOTES
HISTORY OF GOLF
OOOOMMMMM
OMMMMM
EAT TO WIN
ZEN
ROCK CHALK
KU
KANSAS
BASKETBALL

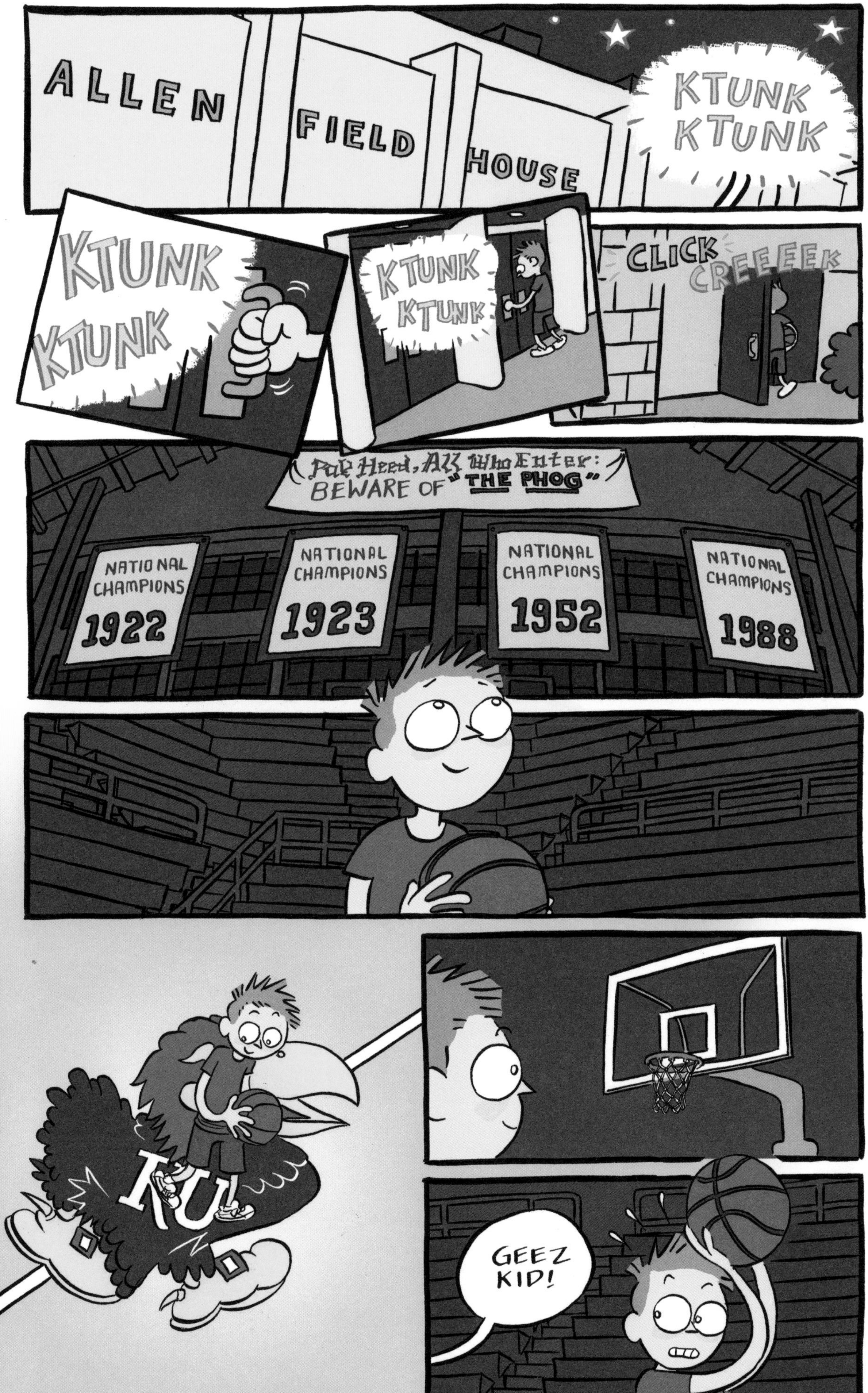
ALLEN FIELD HOUSE
KTUNK KTUNK
KTUNK KTUNK
KTUNK KTUNK
CLICK
CREEEEEK
Pay Heed, All Who Enter: BEWARE OF "THE PHOG"
NATIONAL CHAMPIONS 1922
NATIONAL CHAMPIONS 1923
NATIONAL CHAMPIONS 1952
NATIONAL CHAMPIONS 1988
KU
GEEZ KID!

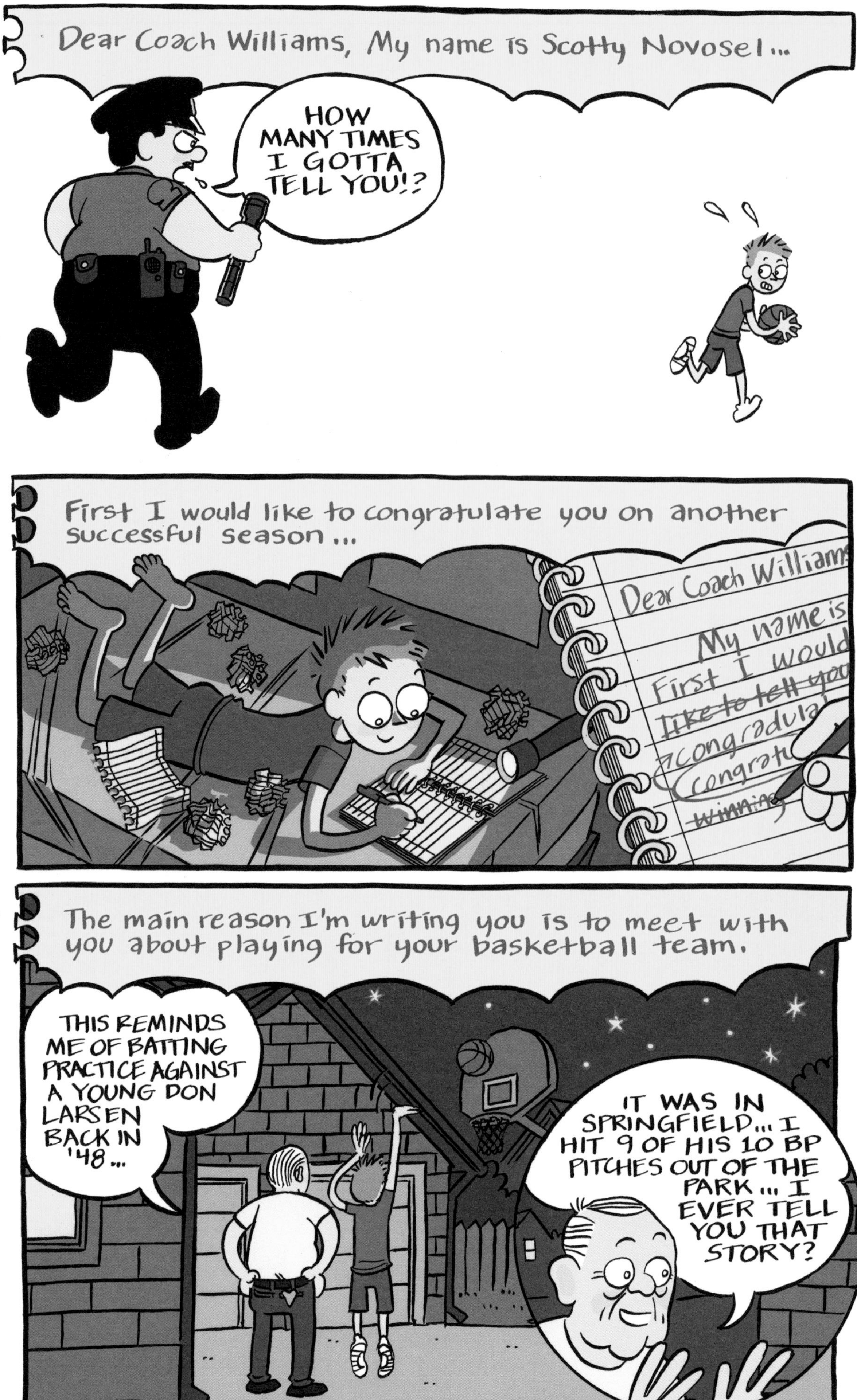
Dear Coach Williams, My name is Scotty Novosel...
HOW MANY TIMES I GOTTA TELL YOU!?
First I would like to congratulate you on another successful season...
Dear Coach Williams
My name is
First I would
like to tell you
congradula
congrat
congrat
winning
The main reason I'm writing you is to meet with you about playing for your basketball team.
THIS REMINDS ME OF BATTING PRACTICE AGAINST A YOUNG DON LARSEN BACK IN '48...
IT WAS IN SPRINGFIELD... I HIT 9 OF HIS 10 BP PITCHES OUT OF THE PARK... I EVER TELL YOU THAT STORY?

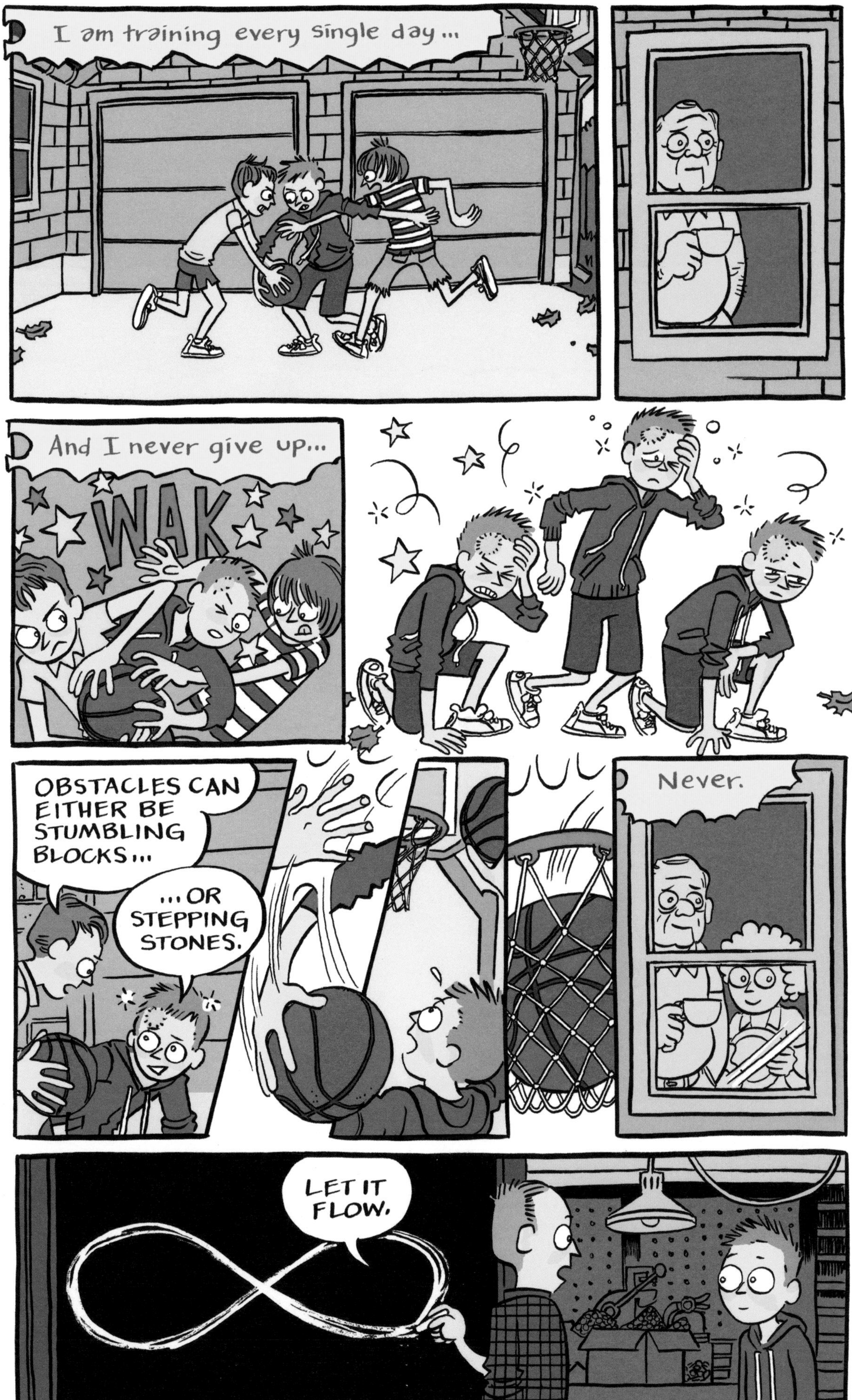
I am training every single day...
And I never give up...
WAK
OBSTACLES CAN EITHER BE STUMBLING BLOCKS...
...OR STEPPING STONES.
Never.
LET IT FLOW.

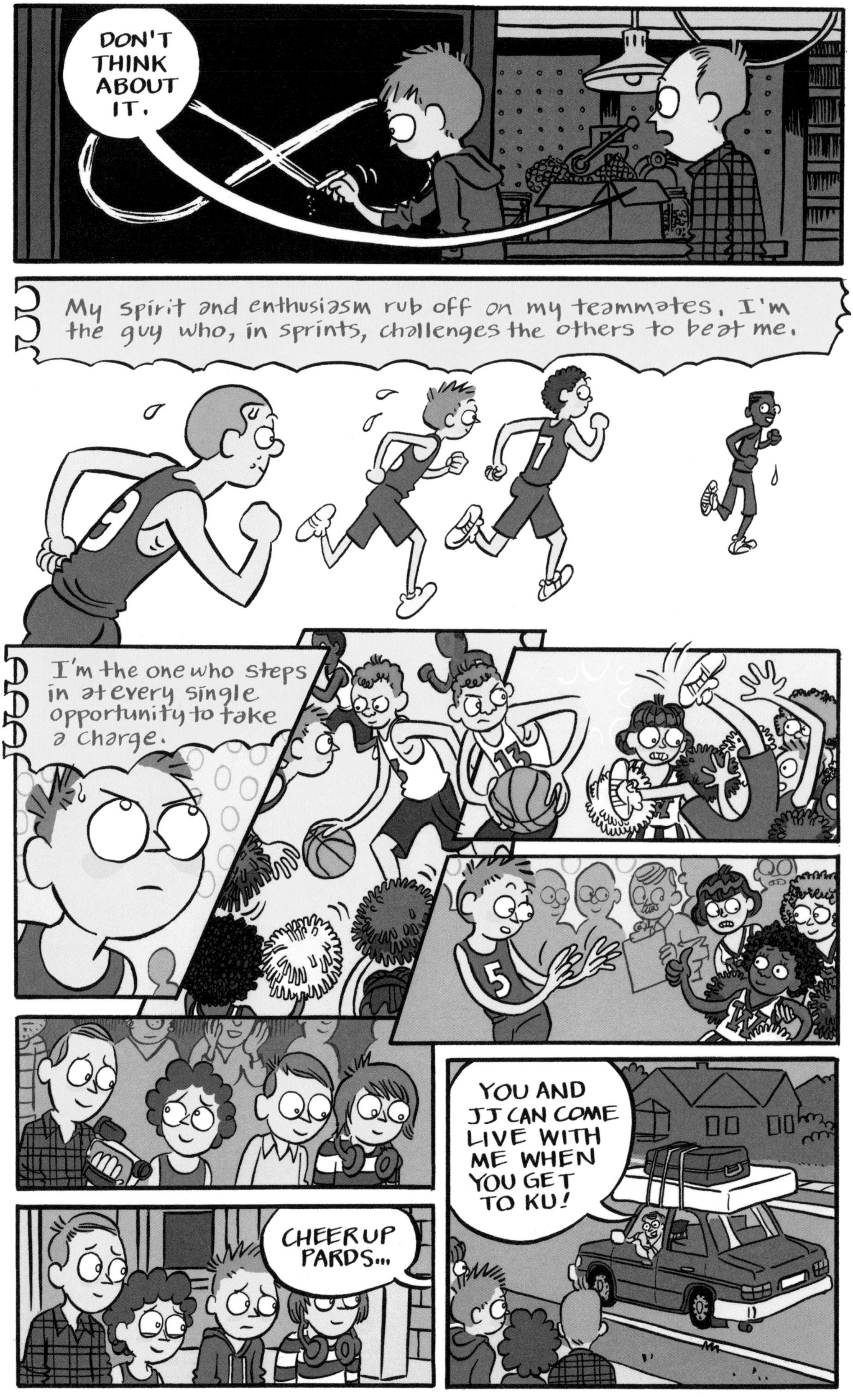
DON'T THINK ABOUT IT.
My spirit and enthusiasm rub off on my teammates. I'm the guy who, in sprints, challenges the others to beat me.
I'm the one who steps in at every single opportunity to take a charge.
CHEER UP PARDS...
YOU AND JJ CAN COME LIVE WITH ME WHEN YOU GET TO KU!

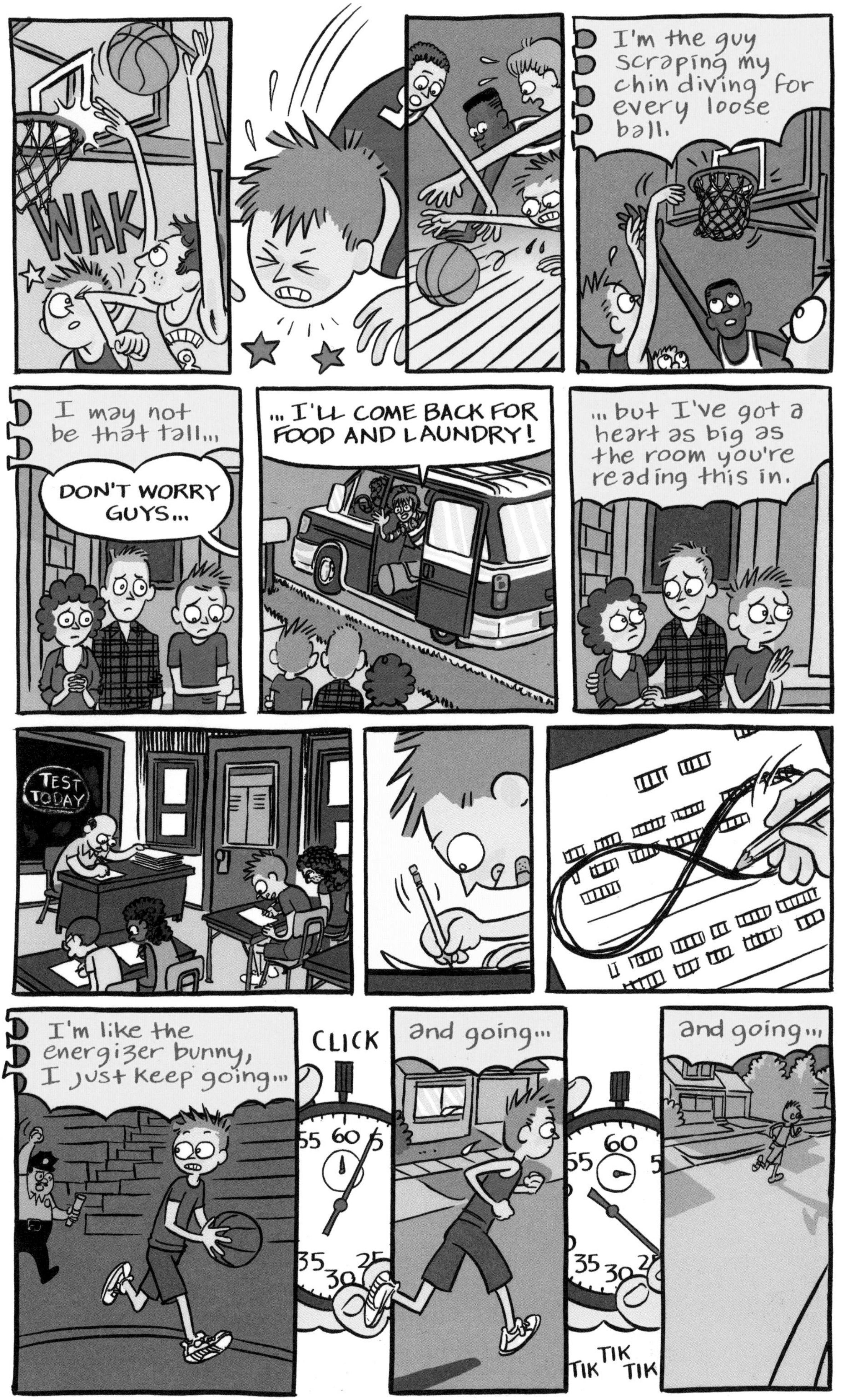
WAK
I'm the guy scraping my chin diving for every loose ball.
I may not be that tall...
DON'T WORRY GUYS...
... I'LL COME BACK FOR FOOD AND LAUNDRY!
... but I've got a heart as big as the room you're reading this in.
TEST TODAY
I'm like the energizer bunny, I just keep going...
CLICK
and going...
TIK TIK TIK
and going...

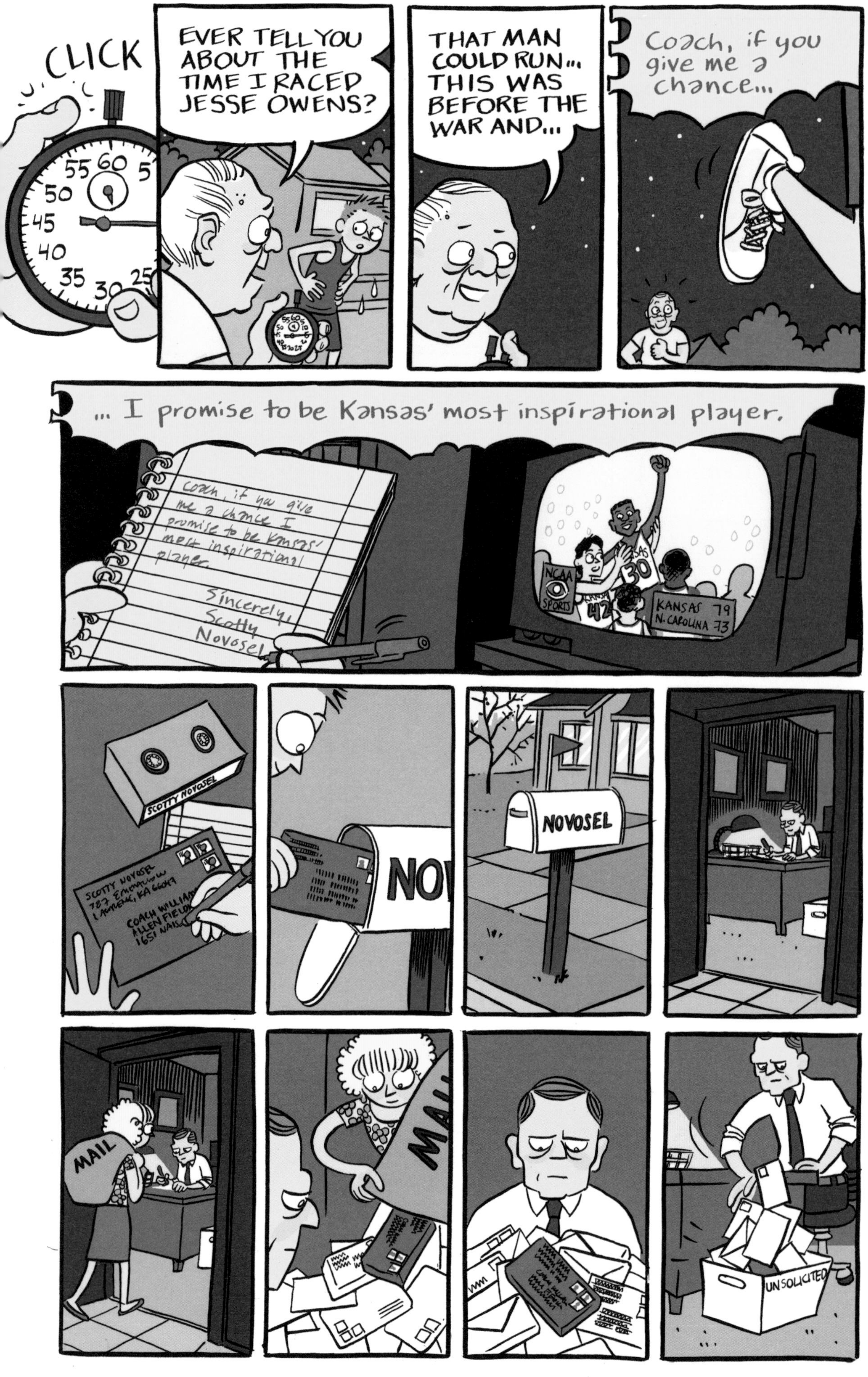

CLICK
EVER TELL YOU ABOUT THE TIME I RACED JESSE OWENS?
THAT MAN COULD RUN... THIS WAS BEFORE THE WAR AND...
Coach, if you give me a chance...
... I promise to be Kansas' most inspirational player.
Coach, if you give me a chance I promise to be Kansas' most inspirational player.
Sincerely, Scotty Novosel
NCAA SPORTS
KANSAS 79
N. CAROLINA 73
SCOTTY NOVOSEL
NOVOSEL
MAIL
UNSOLICITED

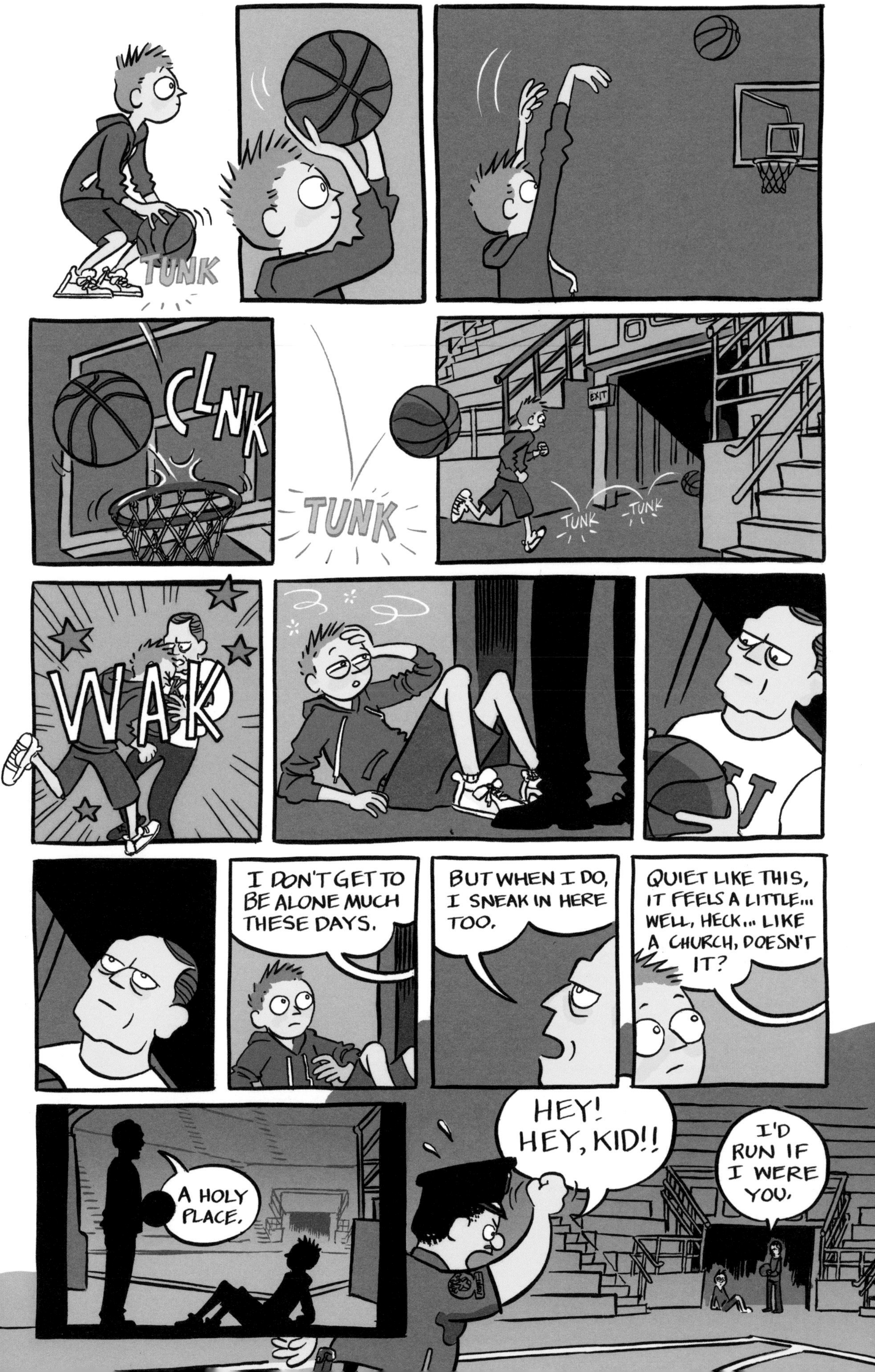
TUNK
CLNK
TUNK
EXIT
TUNK
TUNK
WAK
I DON'T GET TO BE ALONE MUCH THESE DAYS.
BUT WHEN I DO, I SNEAK IN HERE TOO.
QUIET LIKE THIS, IT FEELS A LITTLE... WELL, HECK... LIKE A CHURCH, DOESN'T IT?
A HOLY PLACE.
HEY! HEY, KID!!
I'D RUN IF I WERE YOU.

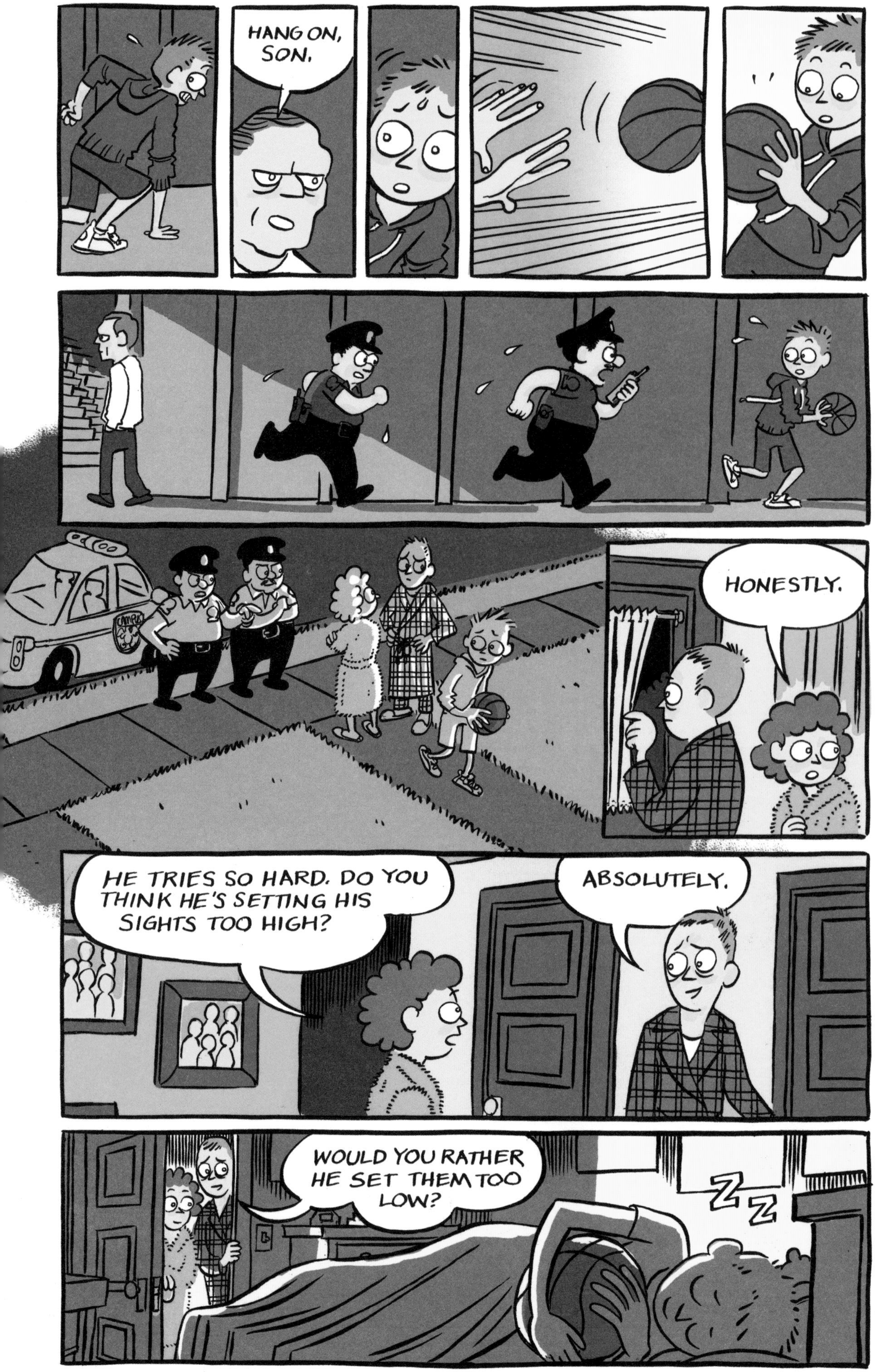
HANG ON, SON.
HONESTLY.
HE TRIES SO HARD. DO YOU THINK HE'S SETTING HIS SIGHTS TOO HIGH?
ABSOLUTELY.
WOULD YOU RATHER HE SET THEM TOO LOW?
Z Z

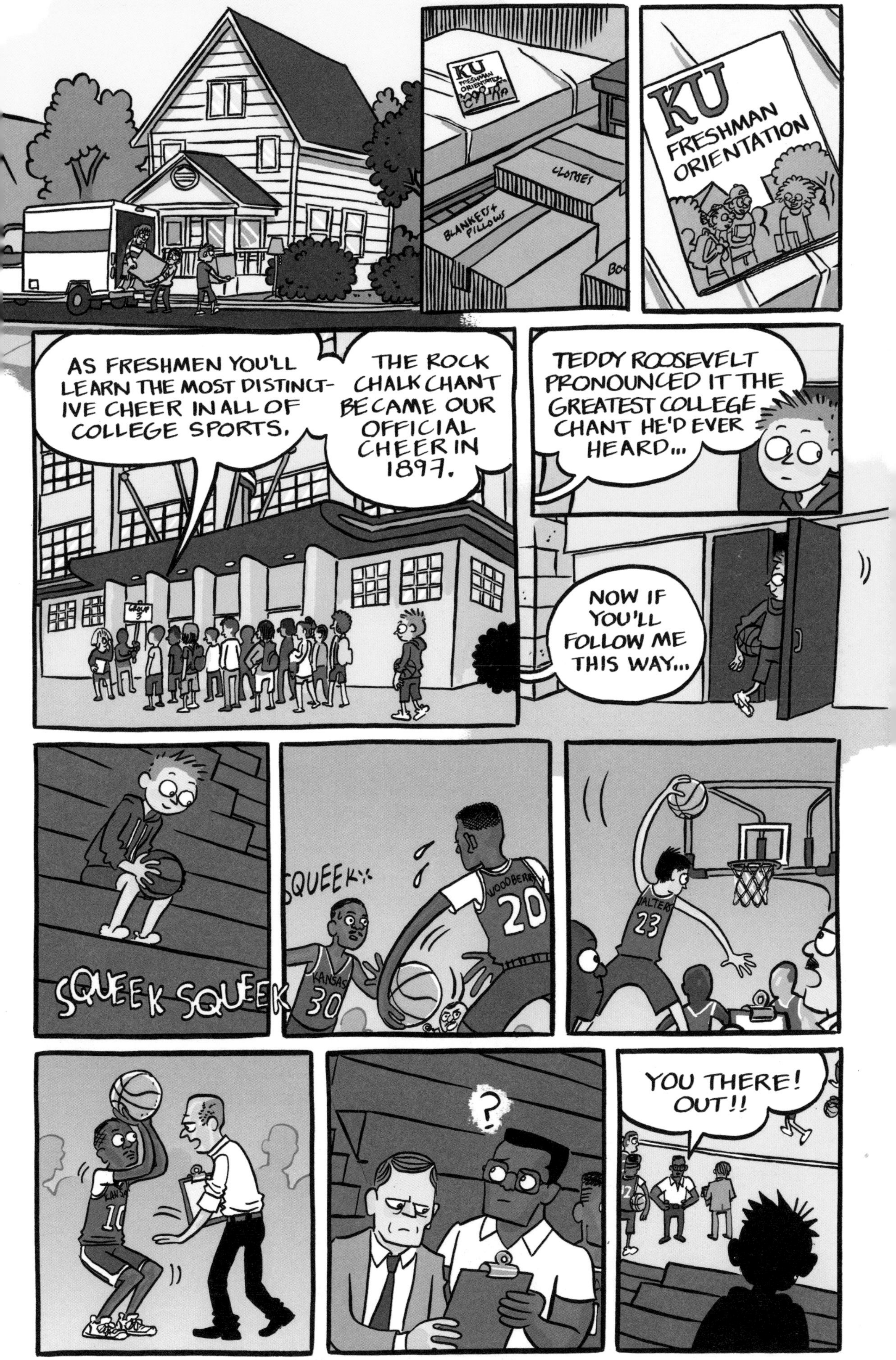
KU FRESHMAN ORIENTATION
CLOTHES
BLANKETS + PILLOWS
KU FRESHMAN ORIENTATION
AS FRESHMEN YOU'LL LEARN THE MOST DISTINCT-IVE CHEER IN ALL OF COLLEGE SPORTS.
THE ROCK CHALK CHANT BECAME OUR OFFICIAL CHEER IN 1897.
GROUP 3
TEDDY ROOSEVELT PRONOUNCED IT THE GREATEST COLLEGE CHANT HE'D EVER HEARD...
NOW IF YOU'LL FOLLOW ME THIS WAY...
SQUEEK SQUEEK
SQUEEK
WOODBERRY 20
KANSAS 30
WALTERS 23
KANSAS 10
?
YOU THERE! OUT!!

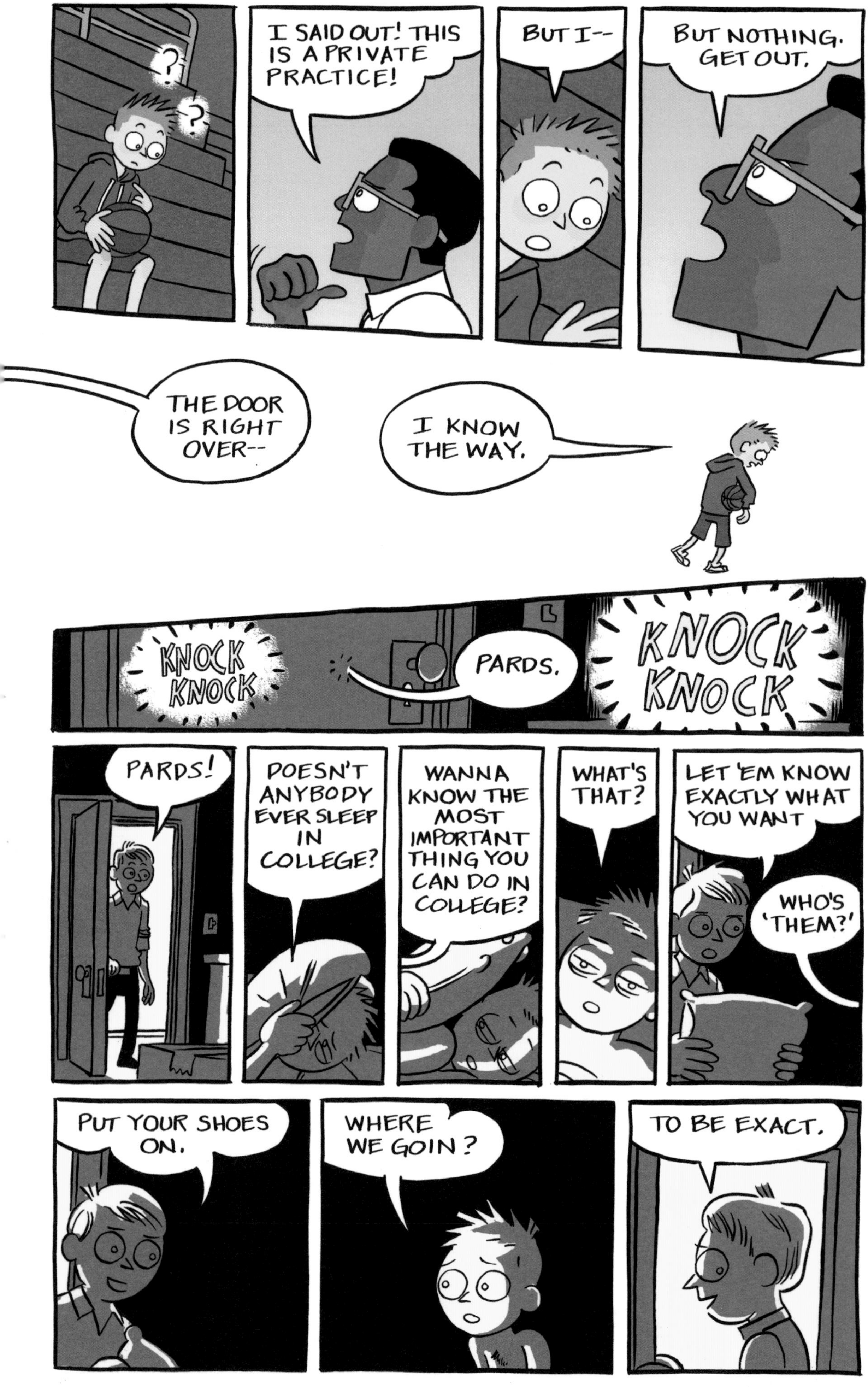
I SAID OUT! THIS IS A PRIVATE PRACTICE!
BUT I--
BUT NOTHING. GET OUT.
THE DOOR IS RIGHT OVER--
I KNOW THE WAY.
KNOCK KNOCK
PARDS.
KNOCK KNOCK
PARDS!
DOESN'T ANYBODY EVER SLEEP IN COLLEGE?
WANNA KNOW THE MOST IMPORTANT THING YOU CAN DO IN COLLEGE?
WHAT'S THAT?
LET 'EM KNOW EXACTLY WHAT YOU WANT
WHO'S 'THEM?'
PUT YOUR SHOES ON.
WHERE WE GOIN?
TO BE EXACT.

BEFORE YOU MOVE A MOUNTAIN YOU MUST FIRST BEGIN BY...

... MOVING STONES.

BEFORE THIS JOURNEY CAN CONTINUE, YOU MUST BEGIN BY TELLING THE UNIVERSE EXACTLY WHAT YOU WANT.

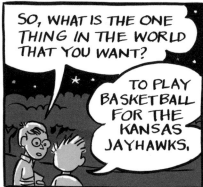

SO, WHAT IS THE ONE THING IN THE WORLD THAT YOU WANT?

TO PLAY BASKETBALL FOR THE KANSAS JAYHAWKS.

DON'T TELL ME PARDS...

... TELL THE UNIVERSE.

I WANT TO WEAR KANSAS ACROSS MY CHEST!

LIKE YOU MEAN IT!

I WANT TO WEAR KANSAS ACROSS MY CHEST!

WHY?

TO REPRESENT THOSE BEFORE ME, THOSE AFTER ME, AND THE CURRENT KU TRADITION!!

AND NOW YOU END WITH THE SOUND OF MANIFESTATION

WHICH IS?

THE SOUND "AH."

AH?

AH!

AAAAAAA

AAAAAAAAAAAAAAAAH

GEEZ, DOESN'T ANYBODY EVER SLEEP ON THIS CAMPUS?

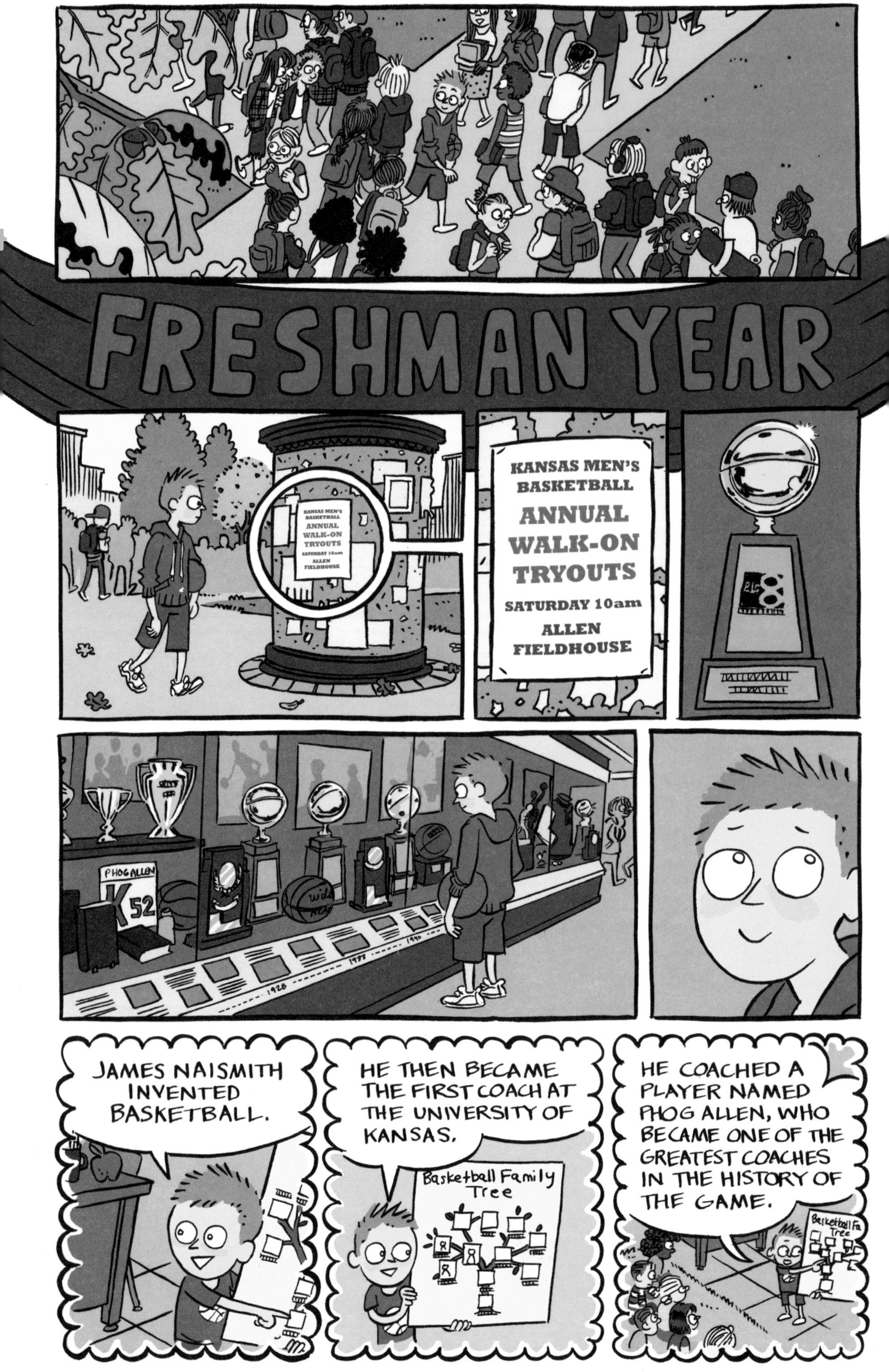
FRESHMAN YEAR
KANSAS MEN'S BASKETBALL
ANNUAL WALK-ON TRYOUTS
SATURDAY 10am
ALLEN FIELDHOUSE
KANSAS MEN'S BASKETBALL
ANNUAL WALK-ON TRYOUTS
SATURDAY 10am
ALLEN FIELDHOUSE
PHOG ALLEN
K 52
JAMES NAISMITH INVENTED BASKETBALL.
HE THEN BECAME THE FIRST COACH AT THE UNIVERSITY OF KANSAS.
Basketball Family Tree
HE COACHED A PLAYER NAMED PHOG ALLEN, WHO BECAME ONE OF THE GREATEST COACHES IN THE HISTORY OF THE GAME.

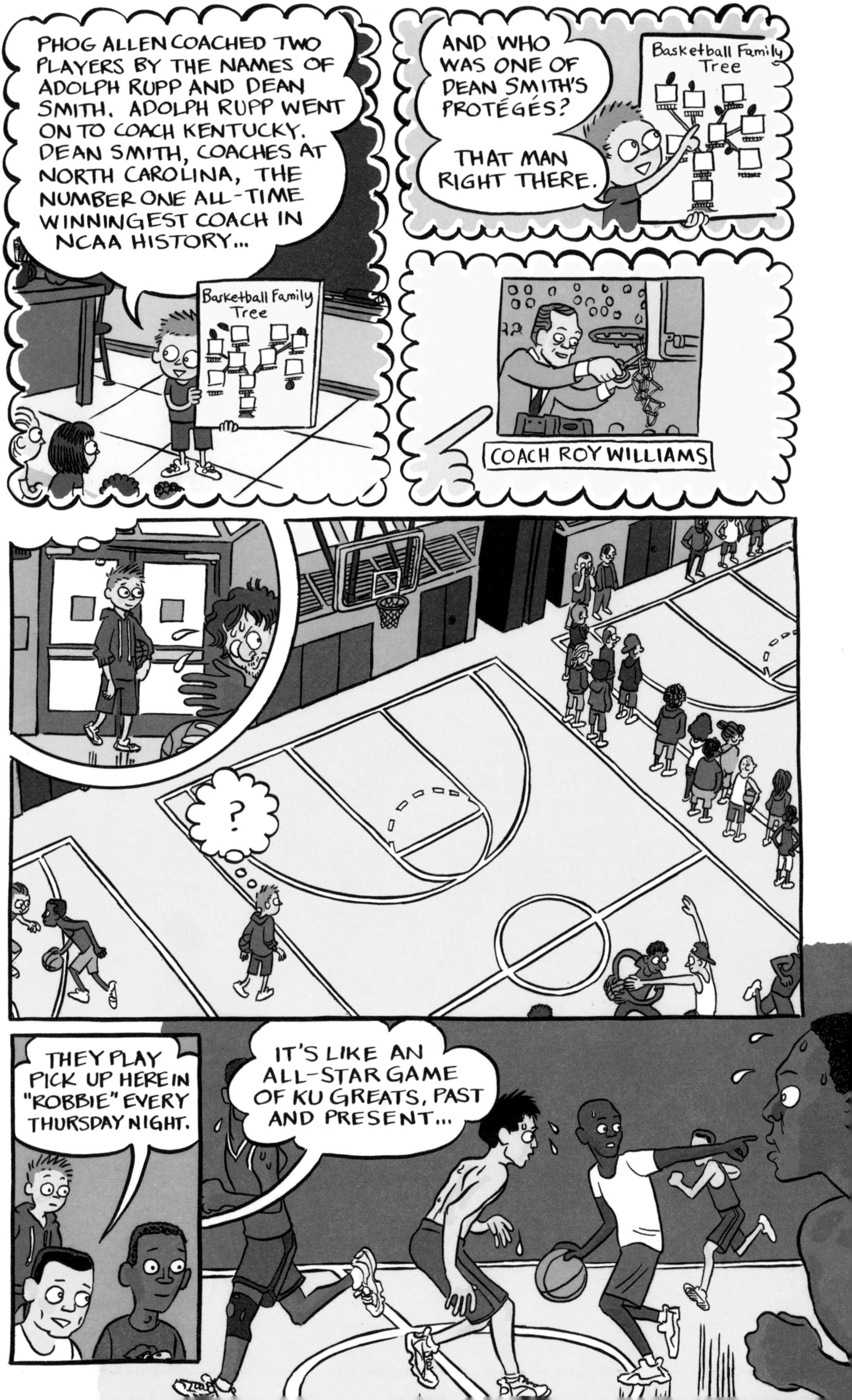
PHOG ALLEN COACHED TWO PLAYERS BY THE NAMES OF ADOLPH RUPP AND DEAN SMITH. ADOLPH RUPP WENT ON TO COACH KENTUCKY. DEAN SMITH, COACHES AT NORTH CAROLINA, THE NUMBER ONE ALL-TIME WINNINGEST COACH IN NCAA HISTORY...
Basketball Family Tree
AND WHO WAS ONE OF DEAN SMITH'S PROTÉGÉS?
THAT MAN RIGHT THERE.
Basketball Family Tree
COACH ROY WILLIAMS
?
THEY PLAY PICK UP HERE IN "ROBBIE" EVERY THURSDAY NIGHT.
IT'S LIKE AN ALL-STAR GAME OF KU GREATS, PAST AND PRESENT...

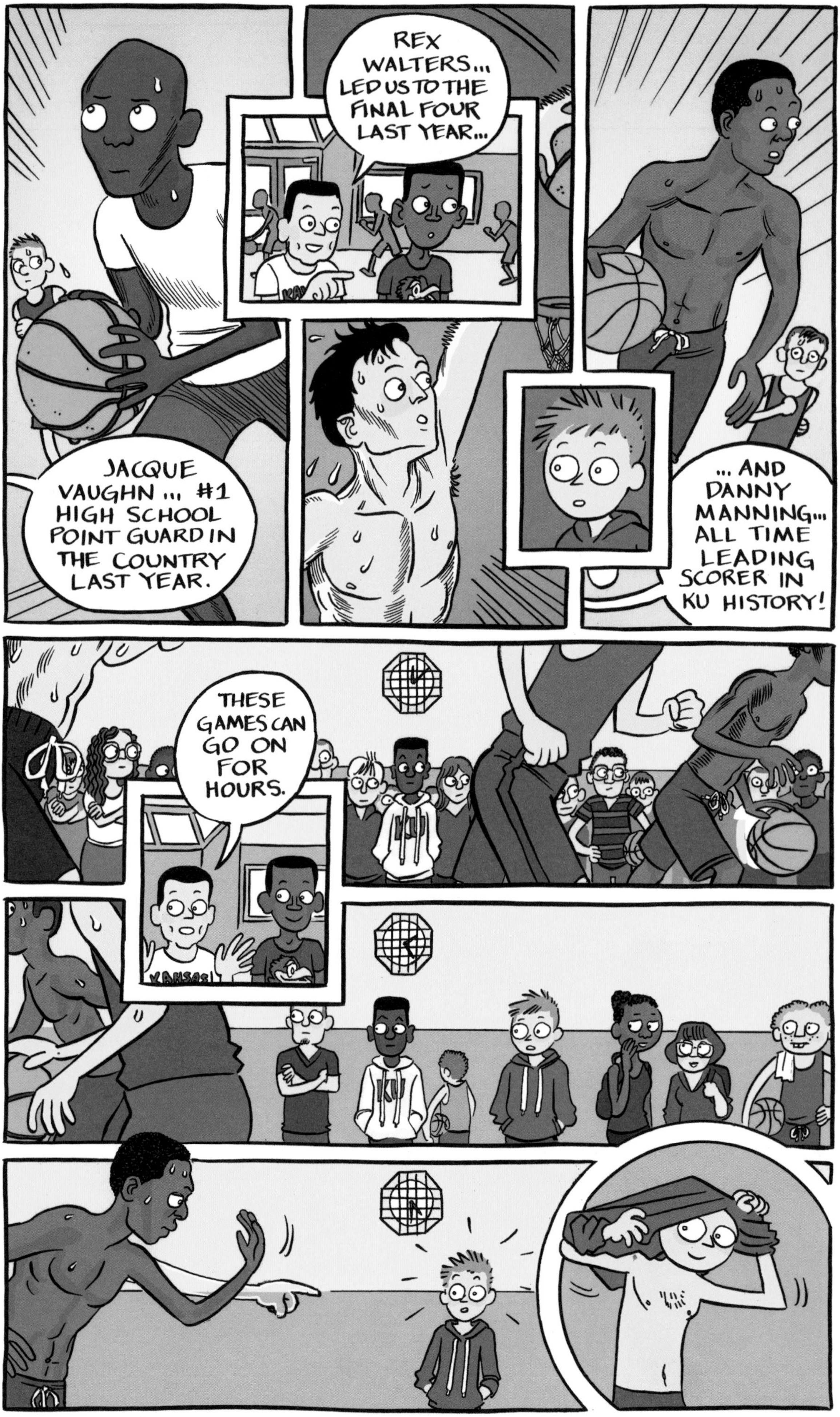
REX WALTERS... LED US TO THE FINAL FOUR LAST YEAR...
JACQUE VAUGHN ... #1 HIGH SCHOOL POINT GUARD IN THE COUNTRY LAST YEAR.
... AND DANNY MANNING... ALL TIME LEADING SCORER IN KU HISTORY!
THESE GAMES CAN GO ON FOR HOURS.
KANSAS!
KU

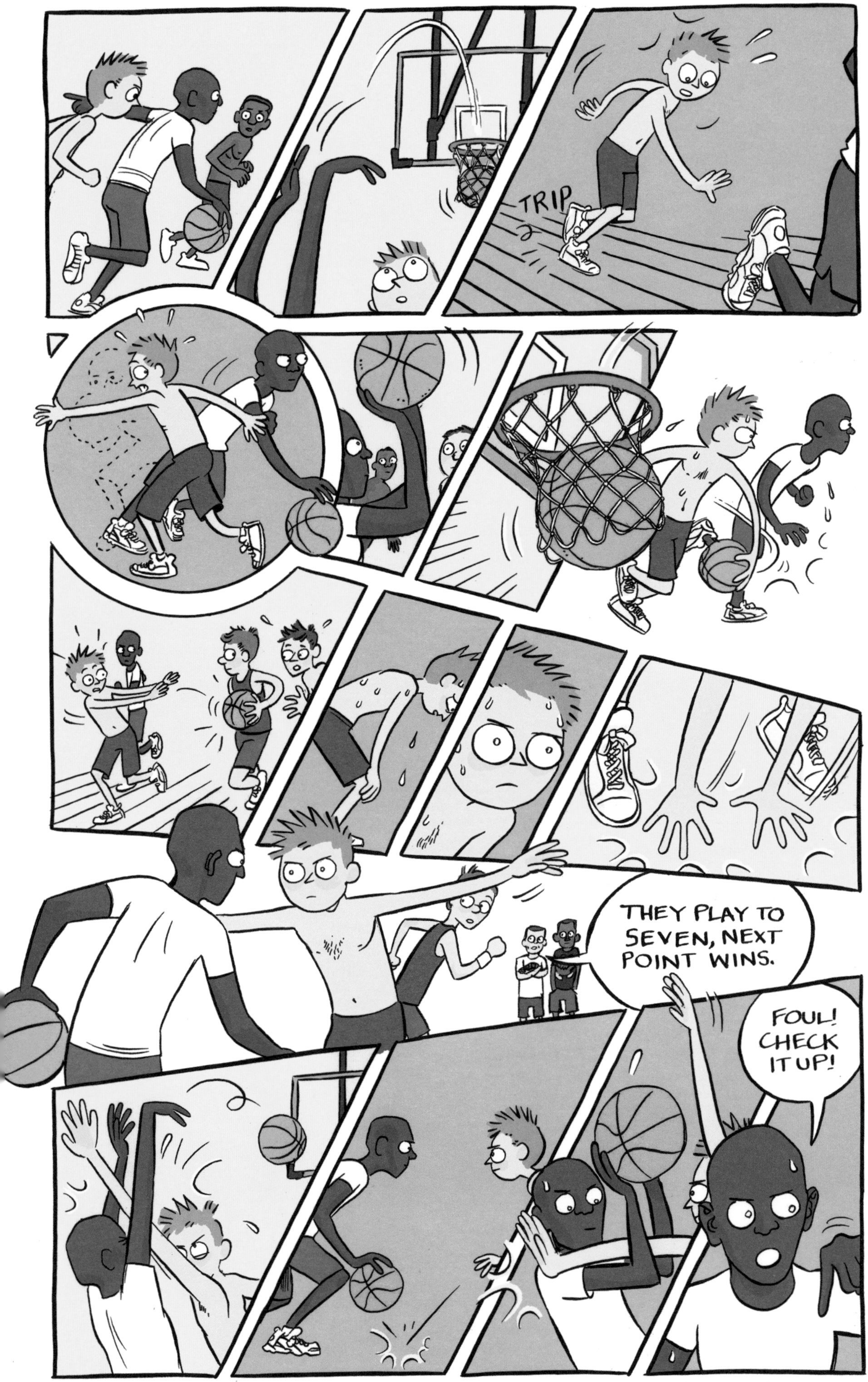
TRIP
THEY PLAY TO SEVEN, NEXT POINT WINS.
FOUL! CHECK IT UP!

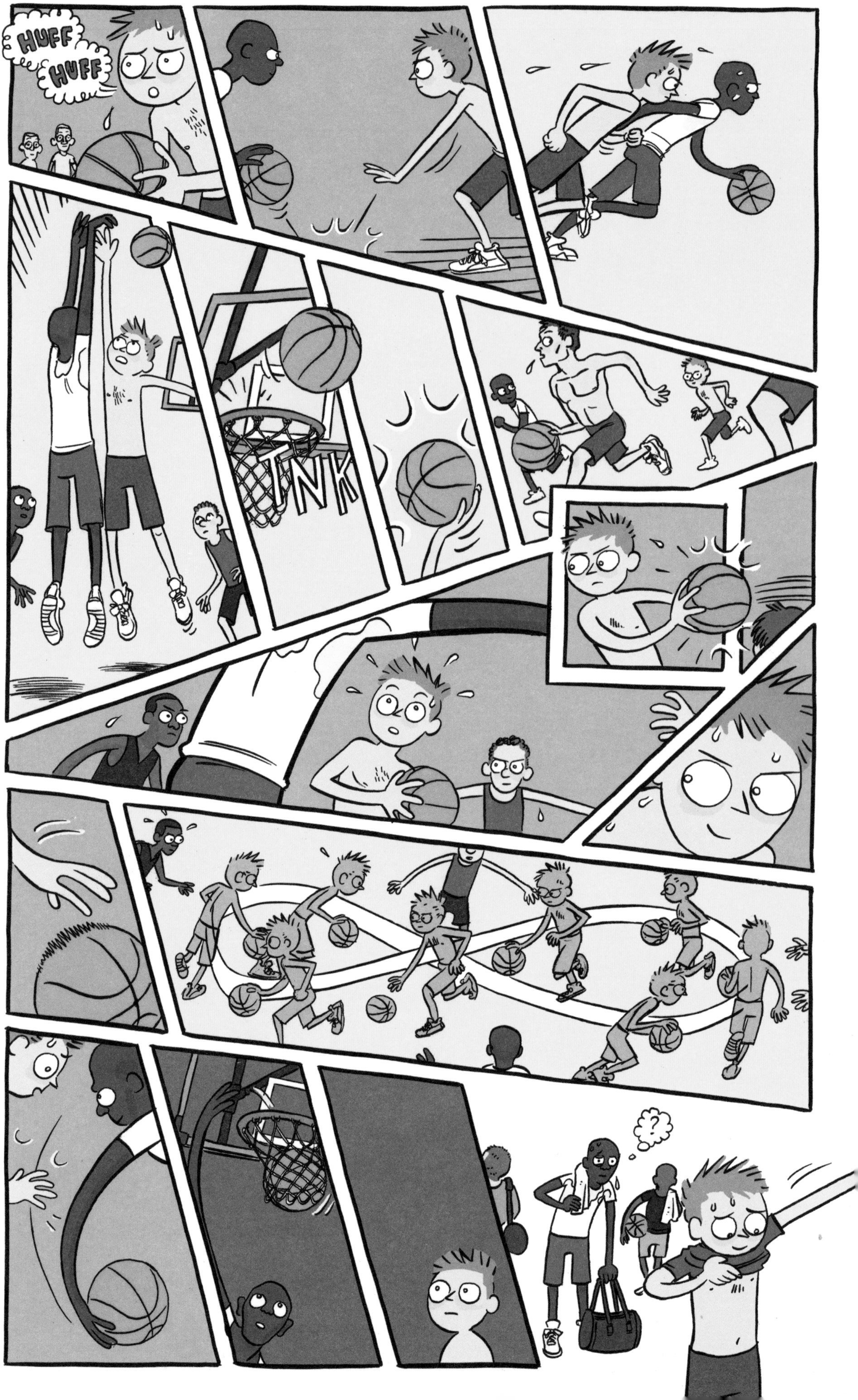
HUFF
HUFF
TNK
?

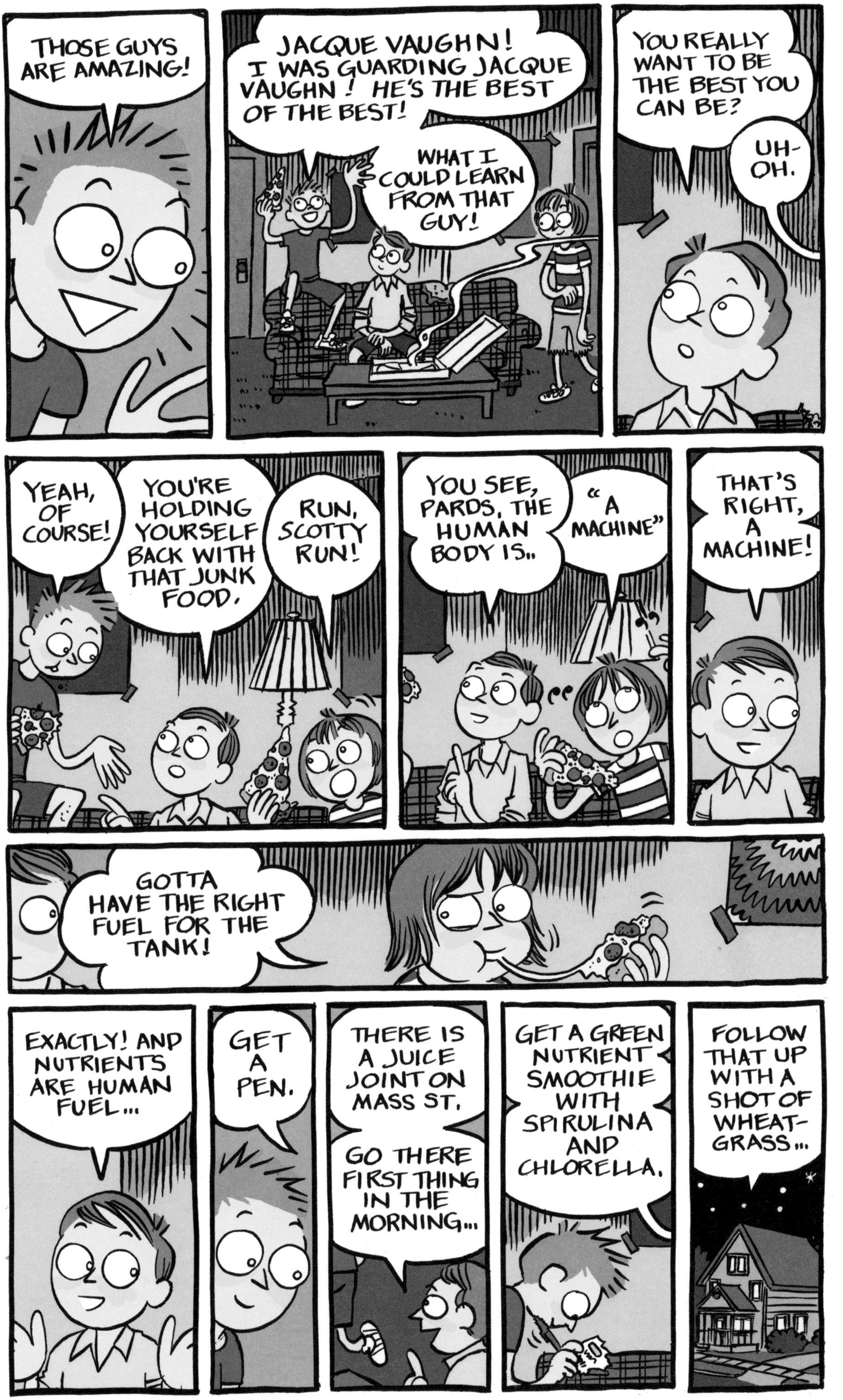
THOSE GUYS ARE AMAZING!
JACQUE VAUGHN! I WAS GUARDING JACQUE VAUGHN! HE'S THE BEST OF THE BEST!
WHAT I COULD LEARN FROM THAT GUY!
YOU REALLY WANT TO BE THE BEST YOU CAN BE?
UH-OH.
YEAH, OF COURSE!
YOU'RE HOLDING YOURSELF BACK WITH THAT JUNK FOOD.
RUN, SCOTTY RUN!
YOU SEE, PARDS, THE HUMAN BODY IS..
"A MACHINE"
THAT'S RIGHT, A MACHINE!
GOTTA HAVE THE RIGHT FUEL FOR THE TANK!
EXACTLY! AND NUTRIENTS ARE HUMAN FUEL...
GET A PEN.
THERE IS A JUICE JOINT ON MASS ST.
GO THERE FIRST THING IN THE MORNING...
GET A GREEN NUTRIENT SMOOTHIE WITH SPIRULINA AND CHLORELLA.
FOLLOW THAT UP WITH A SHOT OF WHEAT-GRASS...

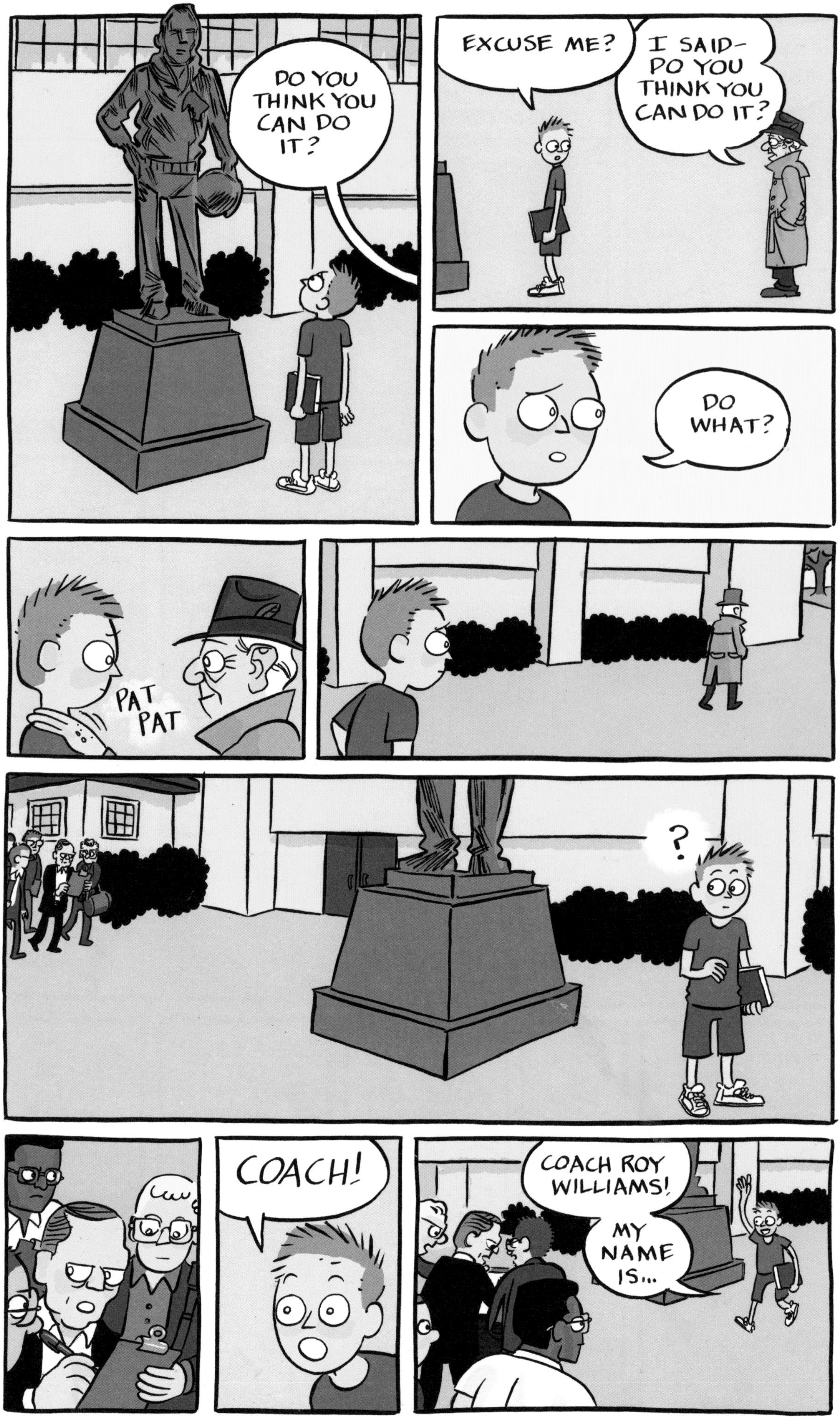

DO YOU THINK YOU CAN DO IT?
EXCUSE ME?
I SAID- DO YOU THINK YOU CAN DO IT?
DO WHAT?
PAT PAT
?
COACH!
COACH ROY WILLIAMS!
MY NAME IS...

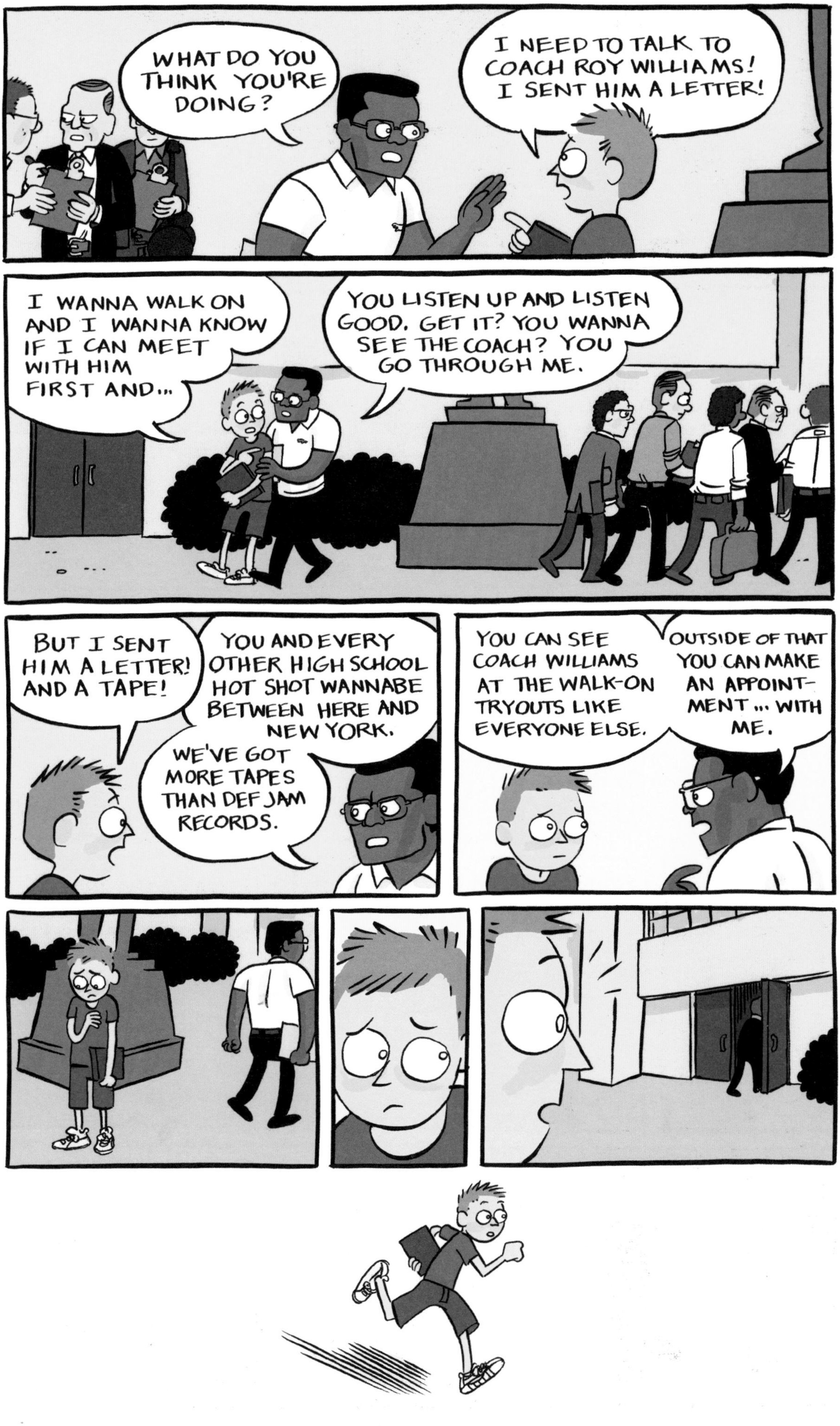
WHAT DO YOU THINK YOU'RE DOING?
I NEED TO TALK TO COACH ROY WILLIAMS! I SENT HIM A LETTER!
I WANNA WALK ON AND I WANNA KNOW IF I CAN MEET WITH HIM FIRST AND...
YOU LISTEN UP AND LISTEN GOOD, GET IT? YOU WANNA SEE THE COACH? YOU GO THROUGH ME.
BUT I SENT HIM A LETTER! AND A TAPE!
YOU AND EVERY OTHER HIGH SCHOOL HOT SHOT WANNABE BETWEEN HERE AND NEW YORK.
WE'VE GOT MORE TAPES THAN DEF JAM RECORDS.
YOU CAN SEE COACH WILLIAMS AT THE WALK-ON TRYOUTS LIKE EVERYONE ELSE.
OUTSIDE OF THAT YOU CAN MAKE AN APPOINT-MENT... WITH ME.

HUFF HUFF
COACH!

YES?

≋HUFF≋ MY NAME IS SCOTTY NOVOSEL AND I WROTE YOU A LETTER ≋HUFF≋ AND I KNOW I'M NOT SUPPOSED TO BOTHER YOU BUT ≋HUFF≋ OH, YEAH, I SENT THIS TAPE, AND, ABOUT THE TRYOUTS ON SATURDAY, I WAS— I MEAN-- I KNOW EVERY OPTION IN YOUR SECONDARY BREAK AND--

TAKE A DEEP BREATH, THERE... EASY DOES IT.

INHALE

IT'S...

...IT'S LIKE A CHURCH.

A HOLY PLACE.

YOU'RE TRYING OUT SATURDAY, HUH?

CAN YOU TELL ME THE VERY FIRST OPTION IN THE SECONDARY BREAK?

GOTTA GET IT INSIDE TO THE BIG MAN... HAVE TO! MAKE THE EASY PLAY LIKE YOU ALWAYS SAY IN THE INTERVIEWS.
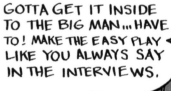

MY OFFICE, FRIDAY, 8:00 AM.

HAVE TO GET IT INSIDE TO THE BIG MAN... MAKE THE EASY PLAY.

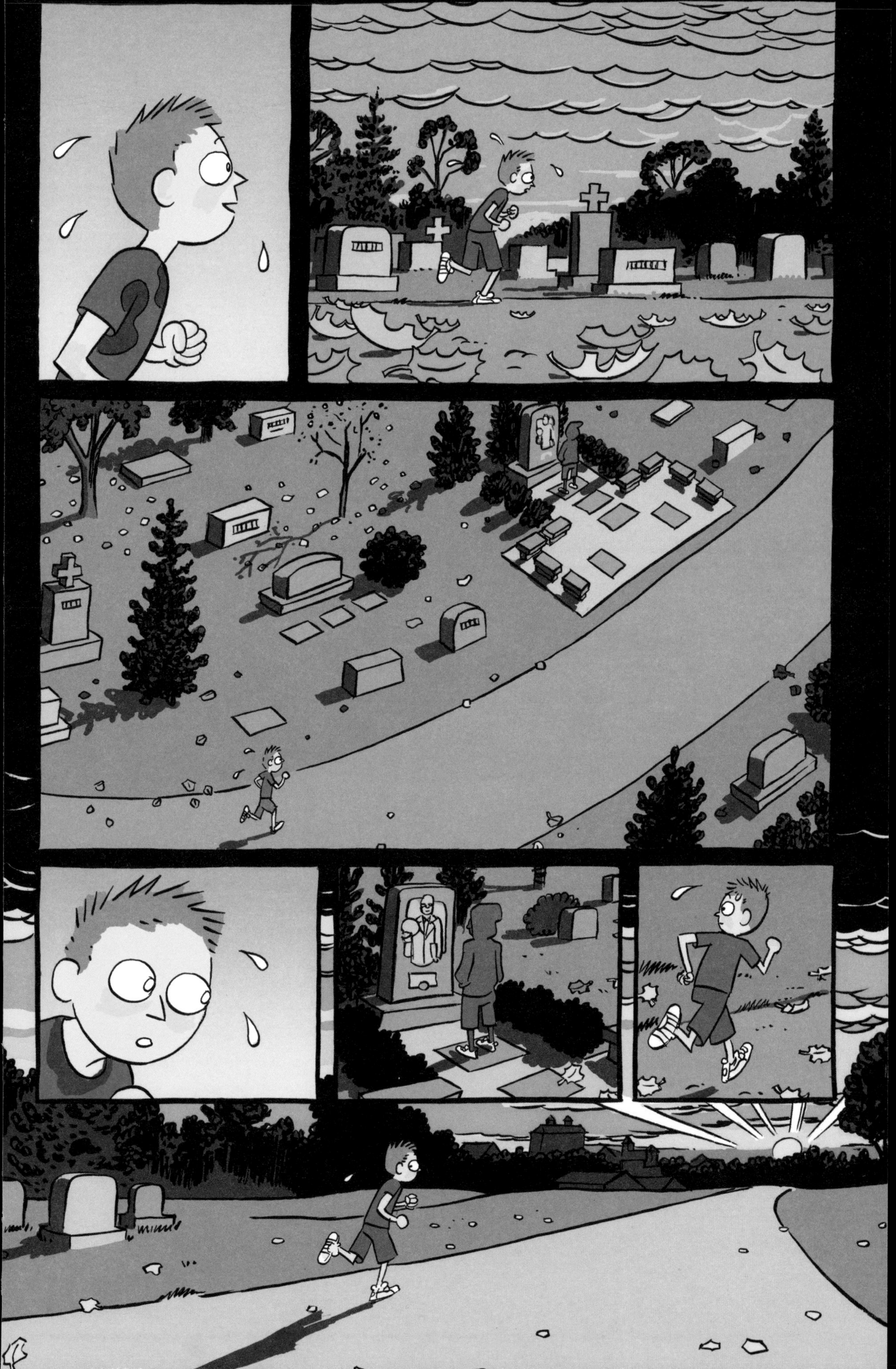

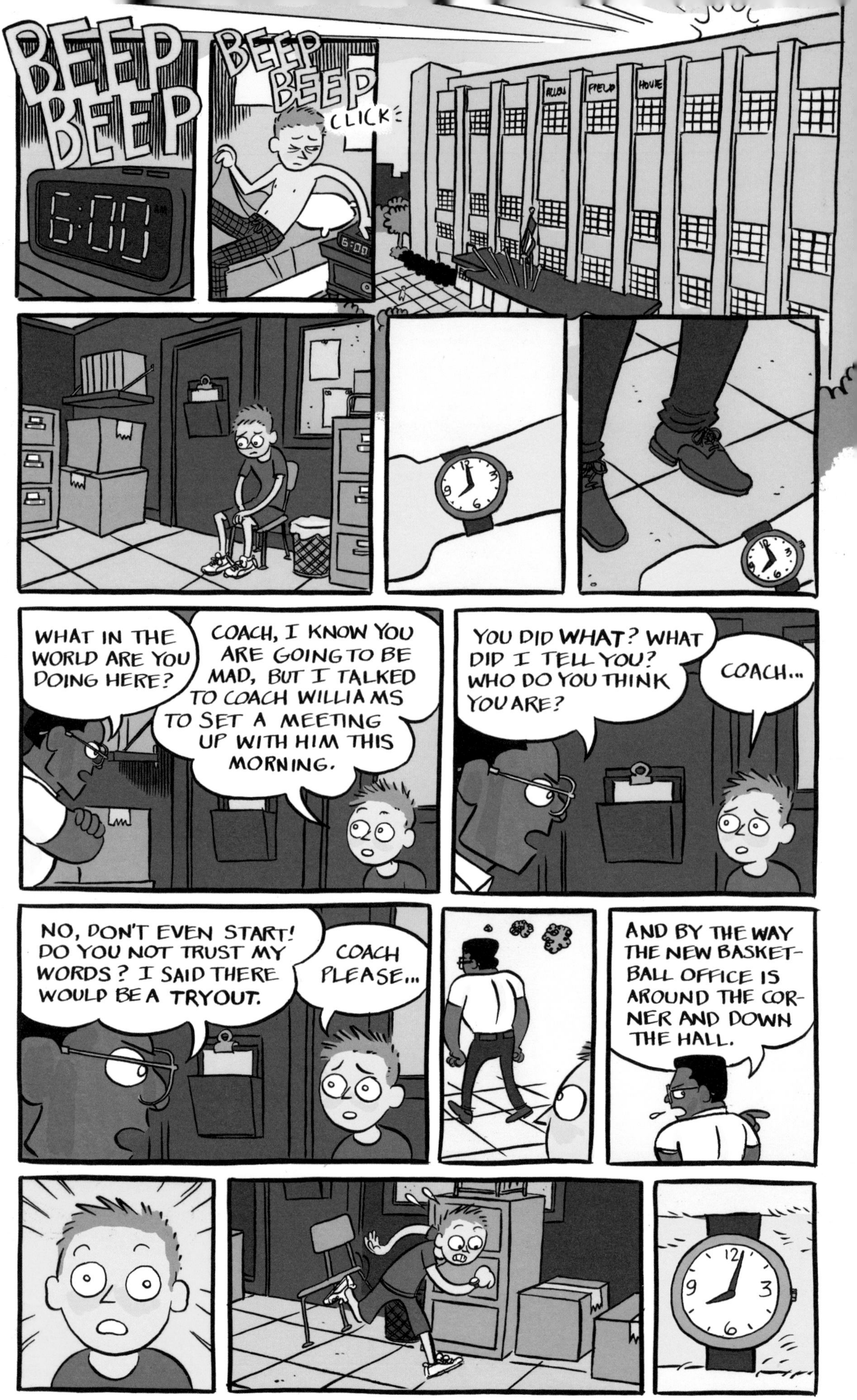

BEEP BEEP
6:00
BEEP BEEP BEEP
CLICK
WHAT IN THE WORLD ARE YOU DOING HERE?
COACH, I KNOW YOU ARE GOING TO BE MAD, BUT I TALKED TO COACH WILLIAMS TO SET A MEETING UP WITH HIM THIS MORNING.
YOU DID WHAT? WHAT DID I TELL YOU? WHO DO YOU THINK YOU ARE?
COACH...
NO, DON'T EVEN START! DO YOU NOT TRUST MY WORDS? I SAID THERE WOULD BE A TRYOUT.
COACH PLEASE...
AND BY THE WAY THE NEW BASKETBALL OFFICE IS AROUND THE CORNER AND DOWN THE HALL.

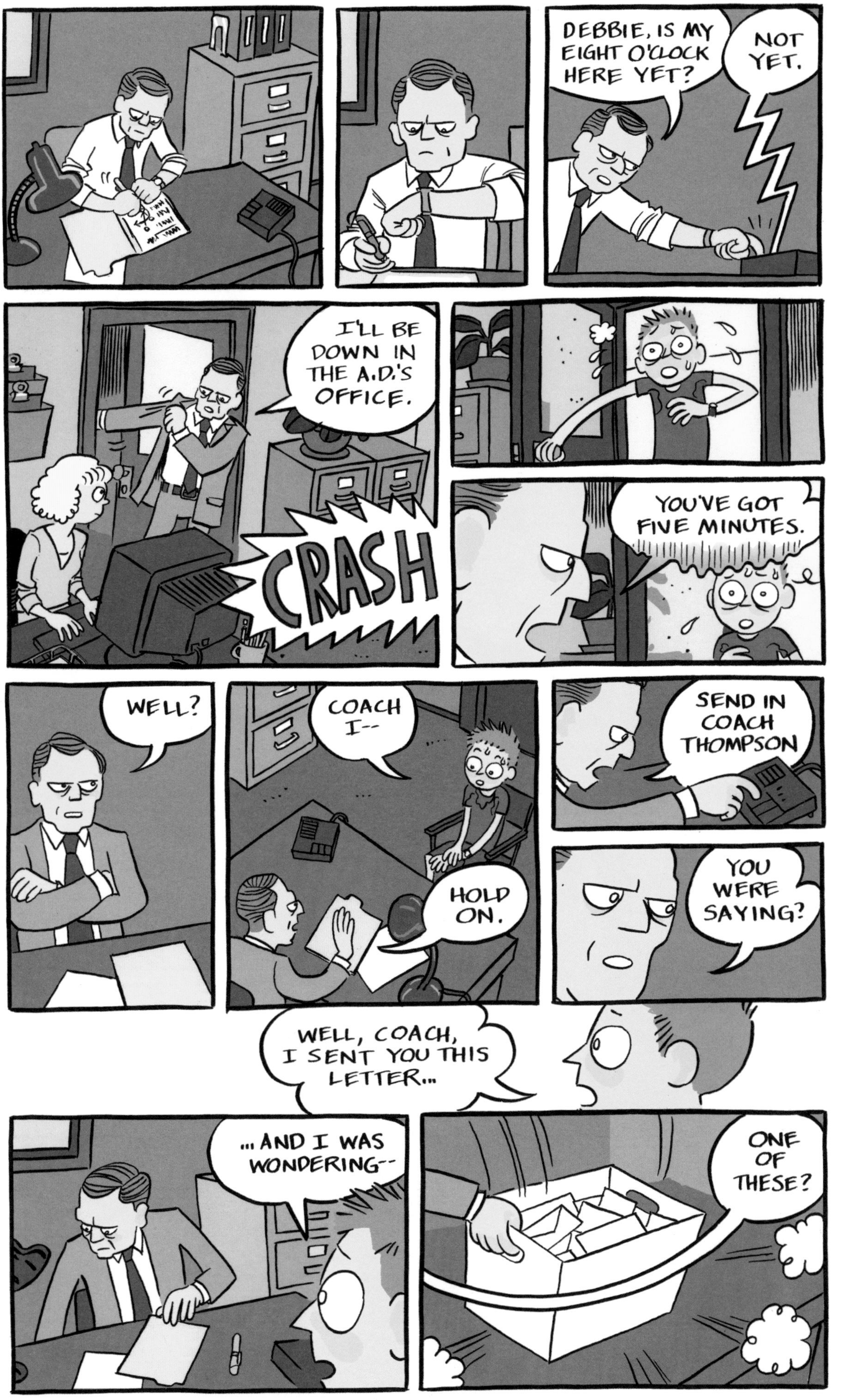
DEBBIE, IS MY EIGHT O'CLOCK HERE YET?
NOT YET.
I'LL BE DOWN IN THE A.D.'S OFFICE.
CRASH
YOU'VE GOT FIVE MINUTES.
WELL?
COACH I--
HOLD ON.
SEND IN COACH THOMPSON
YOU WERE SAYING?
WELL, COACH, I SENT YOU THIS LETTER...
...AND I WAS WONDERING--
ONE OF THESE?

SON, LETS GET TWO THINGS STRAIGHT RIGHT NOW.

WHEN I SAY EIGHT O'CLOCK IT MEANS SEVEN THIRTY...

AND WHEN COACH THOMPSON SAYS PIGS CAN FLY...

YOU BETTER START LOOKING UP.

YOU GET MY MEANING?

YOU GO OVER HIS HEAD AGAIN AND THERE'S NOT A LOT I CAN DO FOR YOU.

THAT BEING SAID, LET ME ASSURE YOU THAT OUR WALK-ON TRYOUTS ARE THE MOST FAIR IN THE THE COUNTRY. IT'S ALL ON THE COURT, AND THERE ISN'T A LETTER OR VIDEOTAPE OR A NOTORIZED ENDORSEMENT FROM WILT CHAMBERLAIN THAT WILL CHANGE WHAT WE SEE OUT THERE TOMORROW.

WILL THERE BE ANYTHING ELSE?

THANK YOU FOR YOUR TIME...

GOOD LUCK HUN.

NOVOSEL, SCOTT

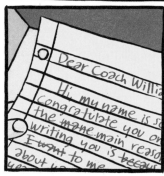
Dear Coach Willi

Hi, my name is s
congratulate you o
the mane main reas
writing you is becaus
I want to me
about

LET'S HOPE HE **SHOOTS** BETTER THAN HE SPELLS.

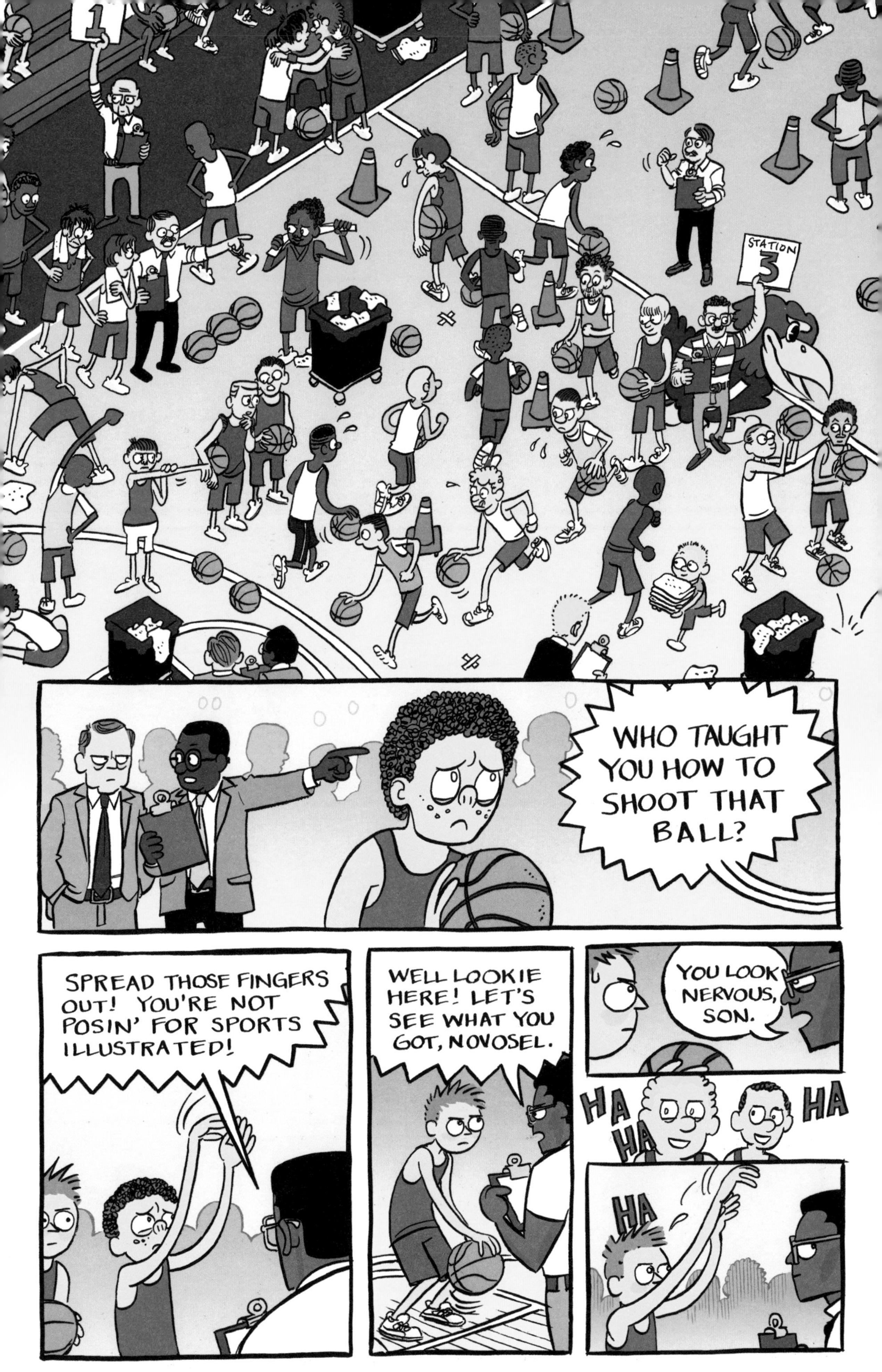
STATION 3
WHO TAUGHT YOU HOW TO SHOOT THAT BALL?
SPREAD THOSE FINGERS OUT! YOU'RE NOT POSIN' FOR SPORTS ILLUSTRATED!
WELL LOOKIE HERE! LET'S SEE WHAT YOU GOT, NOVOSEL.
YOU LOOK NERVOUS, SON.
HA HA HA
HA

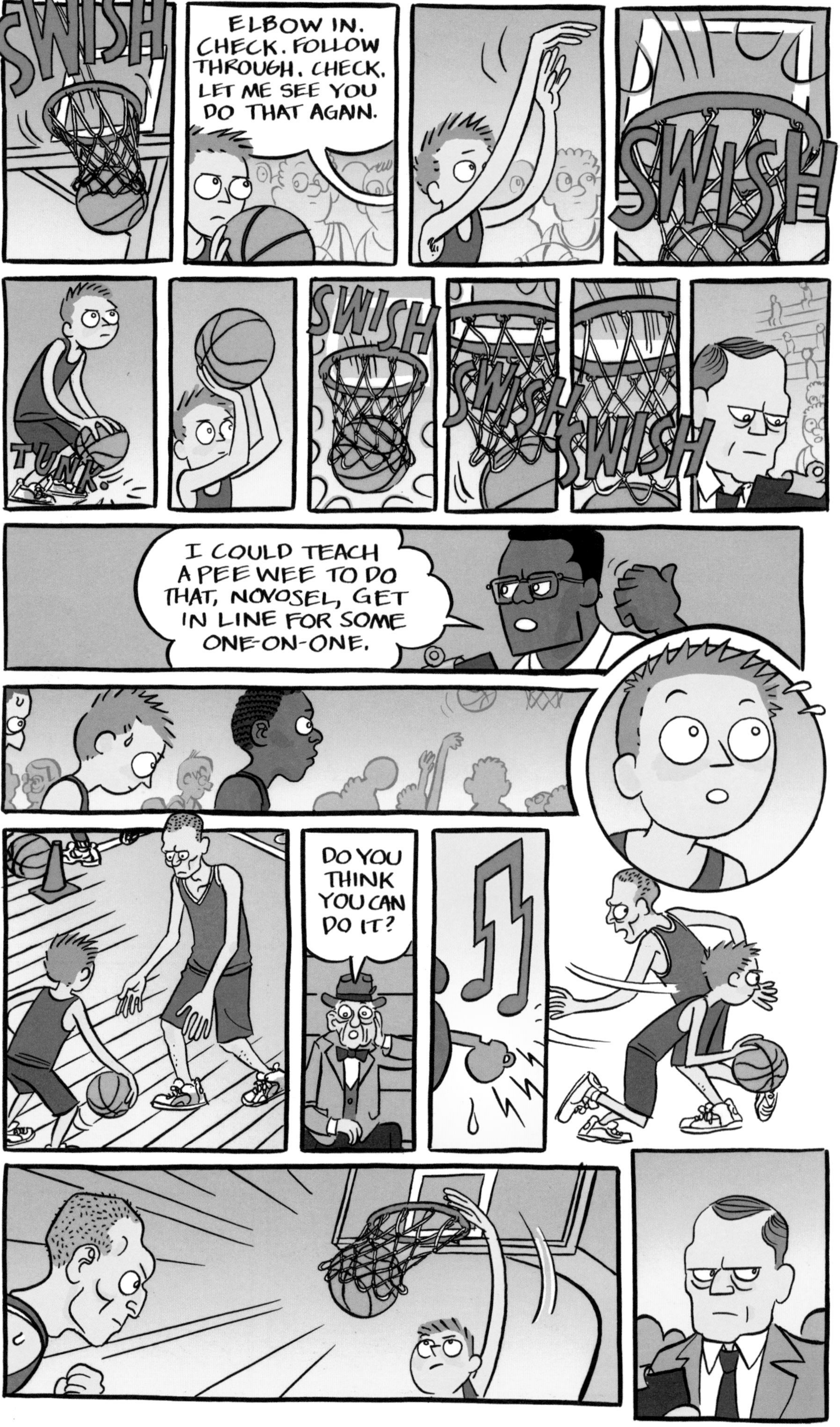
SWISH
ELBOW IN. CHECK. FOLLOW THROUGH. CHECK. LET ME SEE YOU DO THAT AGAIN.
SWISH
TUNK.
SWISH
SWISH
SWISH
I COULD TEACH A PEE WEE TO DO THAT, NOVOSEL. GET IN LINE FOR SOME ONE-ON-ONE.
DO YOU THINK YOU CAN DO IT?

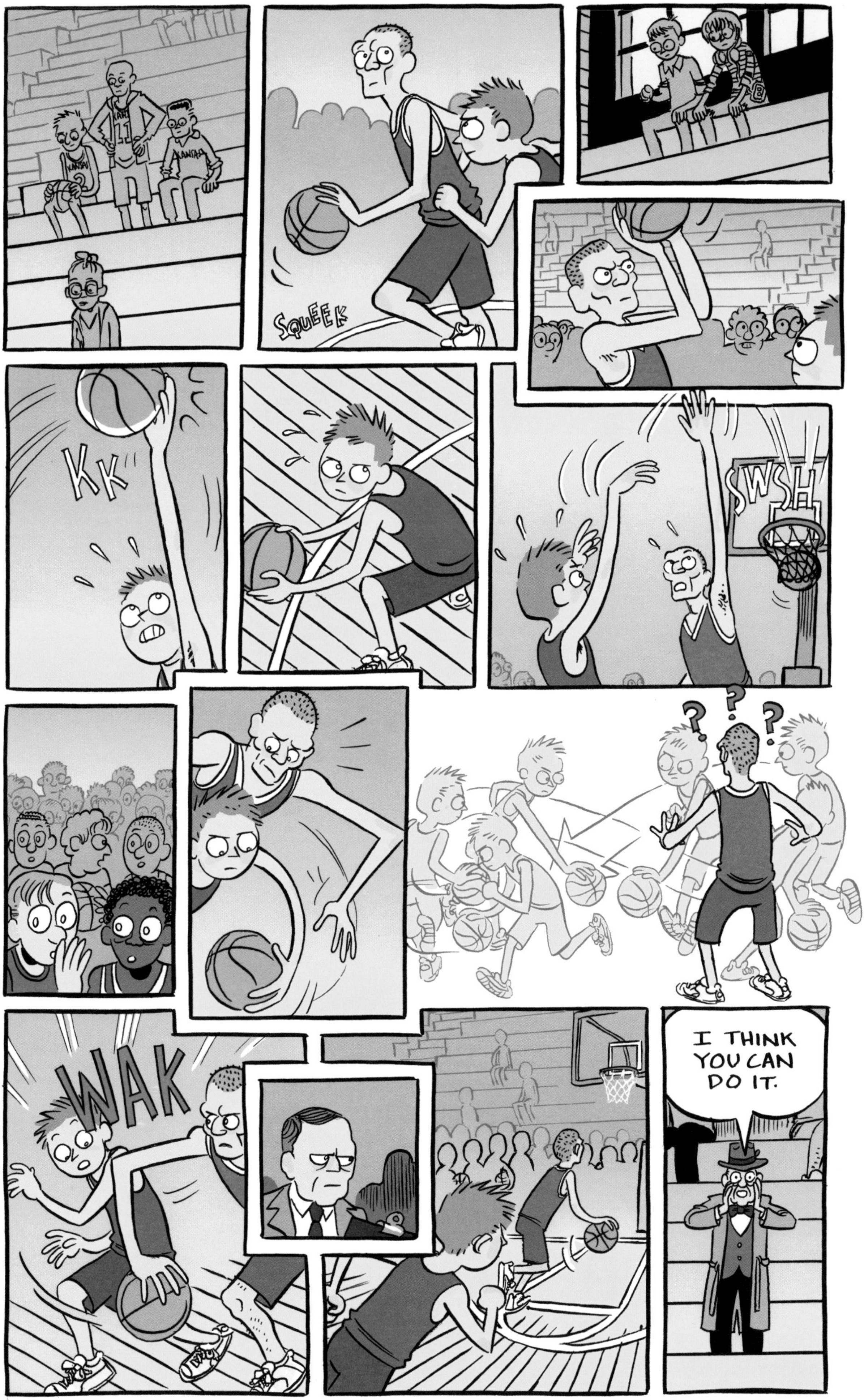
KANSAS
11
KANSAS
SQUEEK
KK
SWSH
? ? ?
WAK
I THINK YOU CAN DO IT.

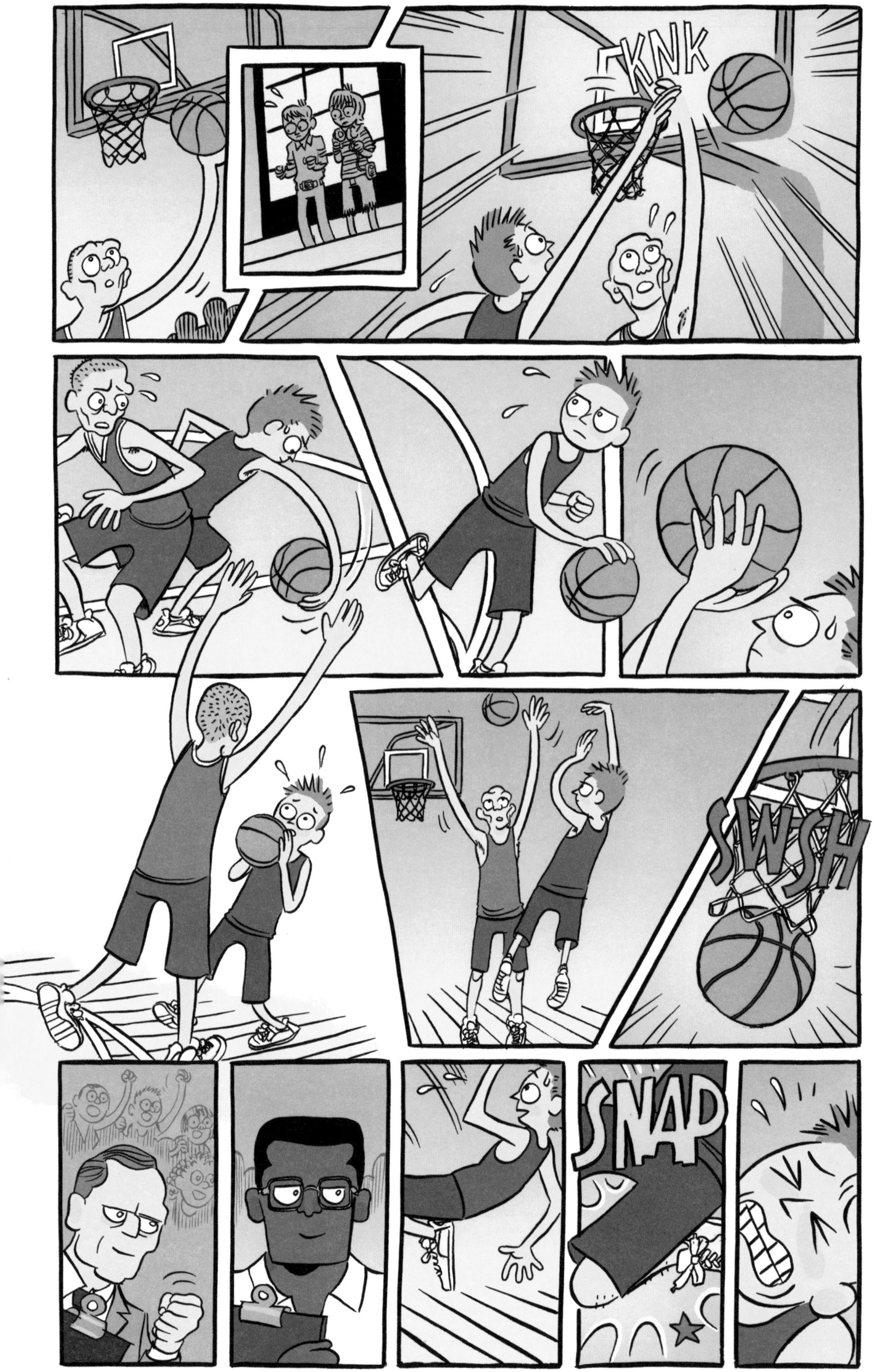
KNK
SWSH
SNAP

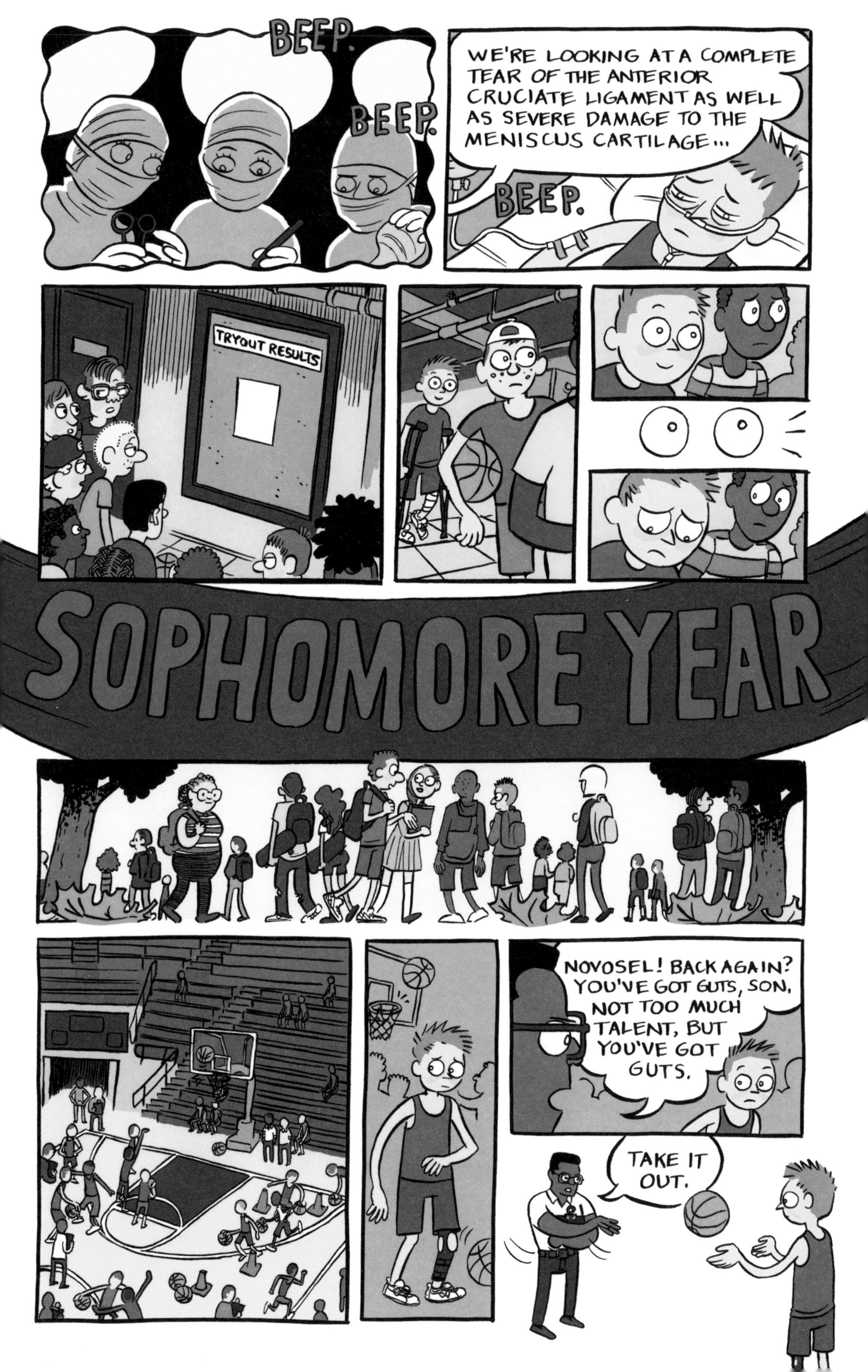
BEEP.
BEEP.
WE'RE LOOKING AT A COMPLETE TEAR OF THE ANTERIOR CRUCIATE LIGAMENT AS WELL AS SEVERE DAMAGE TO THE MENISCUS CARTILAGE...
BEEP.
TRYOUT RESULTS
SOPHOMORE YEAR
NOVOSEL! BACK AGAIN? YOU'VE GOT GUTS, SON, NOT TOO MUCH TALENT, BUT YOU'VE GOT GUTS.
TAKE IT OUT.

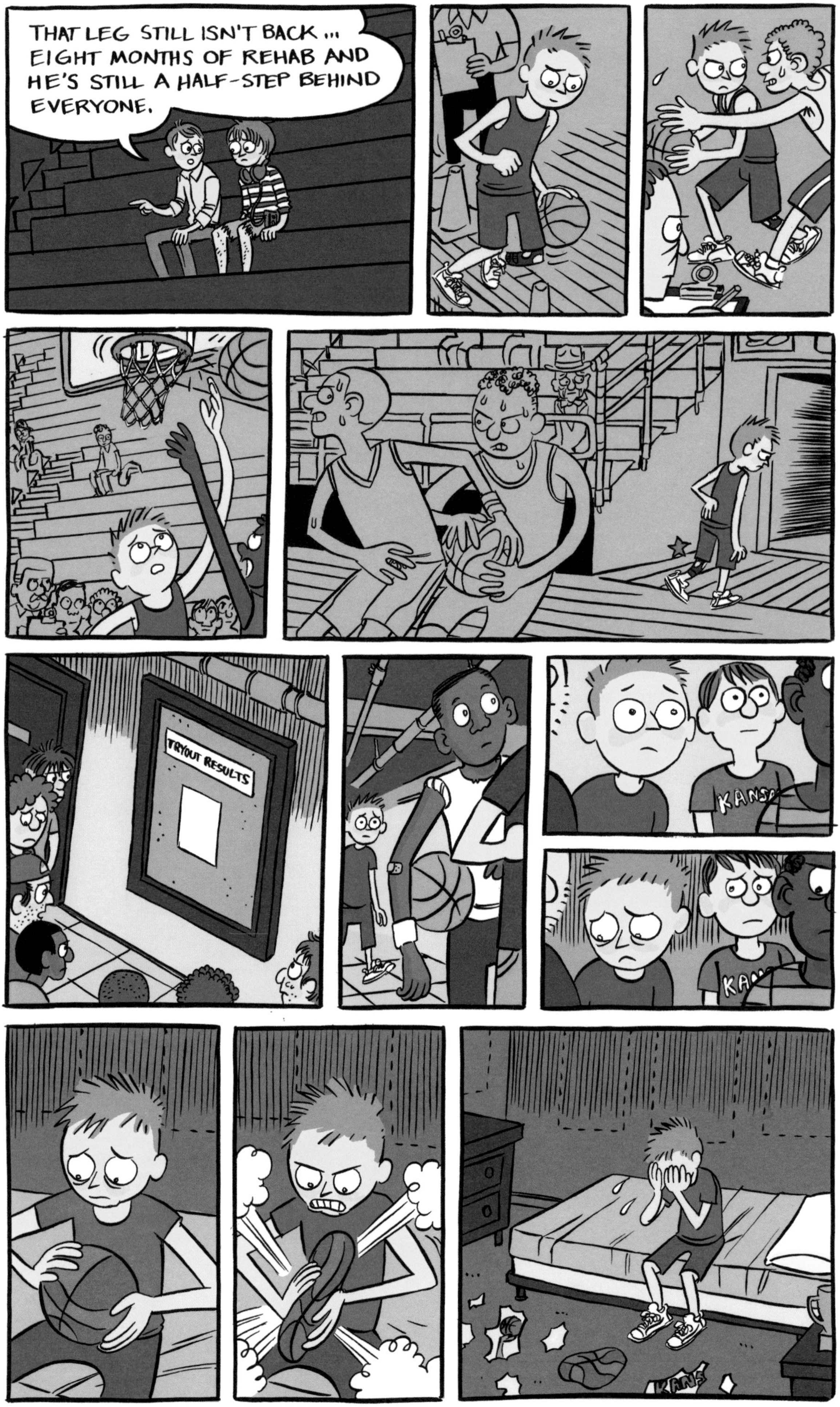
THAT LEG STILL ISN'T BACK... EIGHT MONTHS OF REHAB AND HE'S STILL A HALF-STEP BEHIND EVERYONE.
TRYOUT RESULTS

EVER TELL YOU ABOUT THE TIME I TOOK A LOAD OF SHRAPNEL IN MY LEFT LEG FROM A MORTER IN ALGIERS?

ONLY THE GERMANS DIDN'T CALL IT SHRAPNEL, THEY CALLED IT—

YOU TOLD ME.

DID I?

WELL, NOT LONG AFTER THAT I HAD THAT RACE WITH JESSE OWENS...

I THOUGHT JESSE OWENS WAS BEFORE THE WAR.

HMMM. WAS IT?

YEAH. IT WAS, AND DON LARSEN WAS AFTER THE WAR AND I CAN'T REMEMBER WHEN YOU FOUGHT JOE LOUIS.

WHAT? I NEVER FOUGHT JOE LOUIS!

NO? WELL I FIGURED YOU HAD.

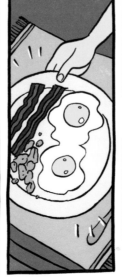

YOU GOT SOMETHING TO SAY SON, YOU BEST SAY IT PLAIN.

SCOTTY, YOU HAVE TO EAT.

PLEASE DON'T TELL ME WHAT I SHOULD DO!

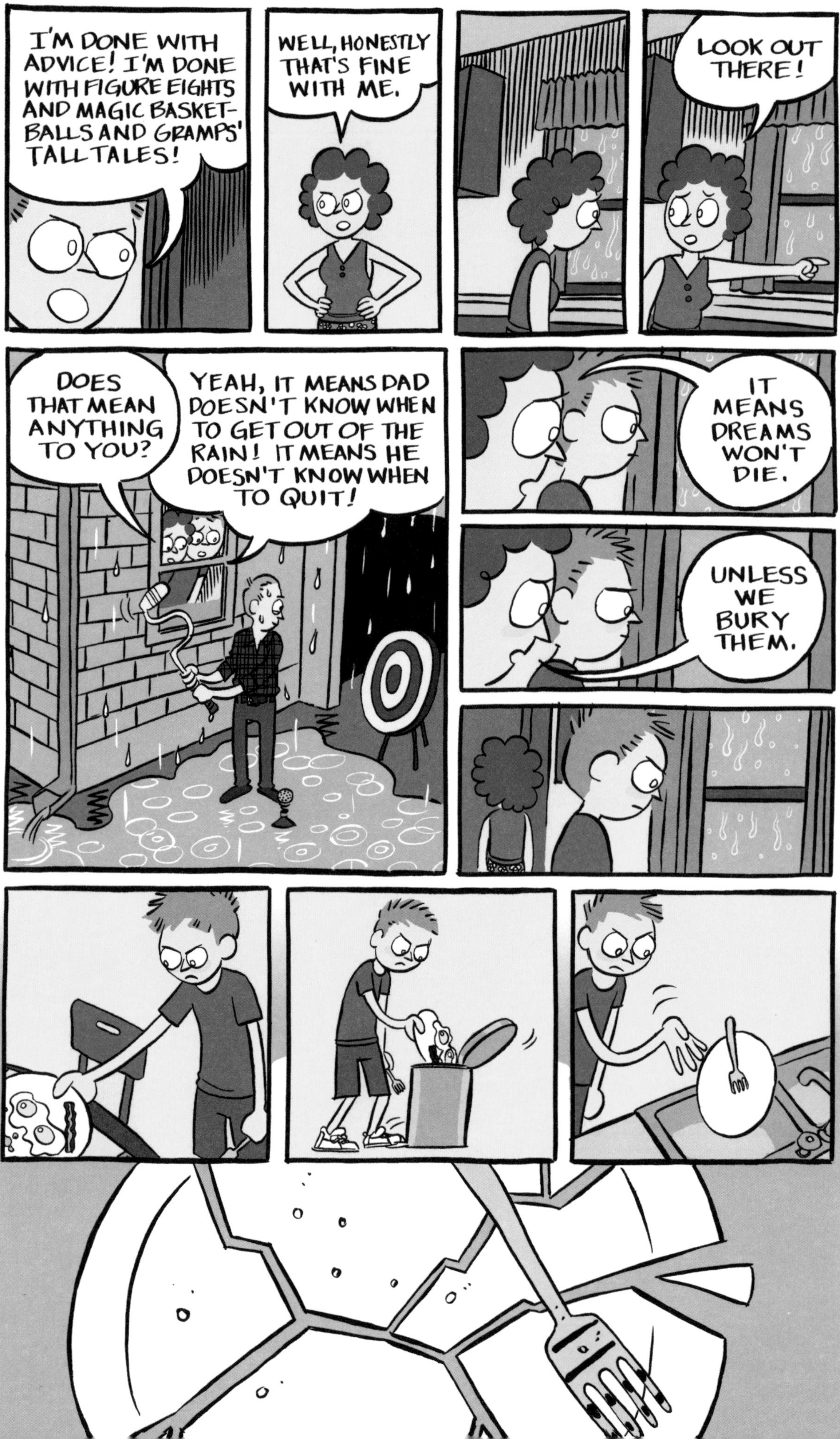
I'M DONE WITH ADVICE! I'M DONE WITH FIGURE EIGHTS AND MAGIC BASKET-BALLS AND GRAMPS' TALL TALES!
WELL, HONESTLY THAT'S FINE WITH ME.
LOOK OUT THERE!
DOES THAT MEAN ANYTHING TO YOU?
YEAH, IT MEANS DAD DOESN'T KNOW WHEN TO GET OUT OF THE RAIN! IT MEANS HE DOESN'T KNOW WHEN TO QUIT!
IT MEANS DREAMS WON'T DIE.
UNLESS WE BURY THEM.

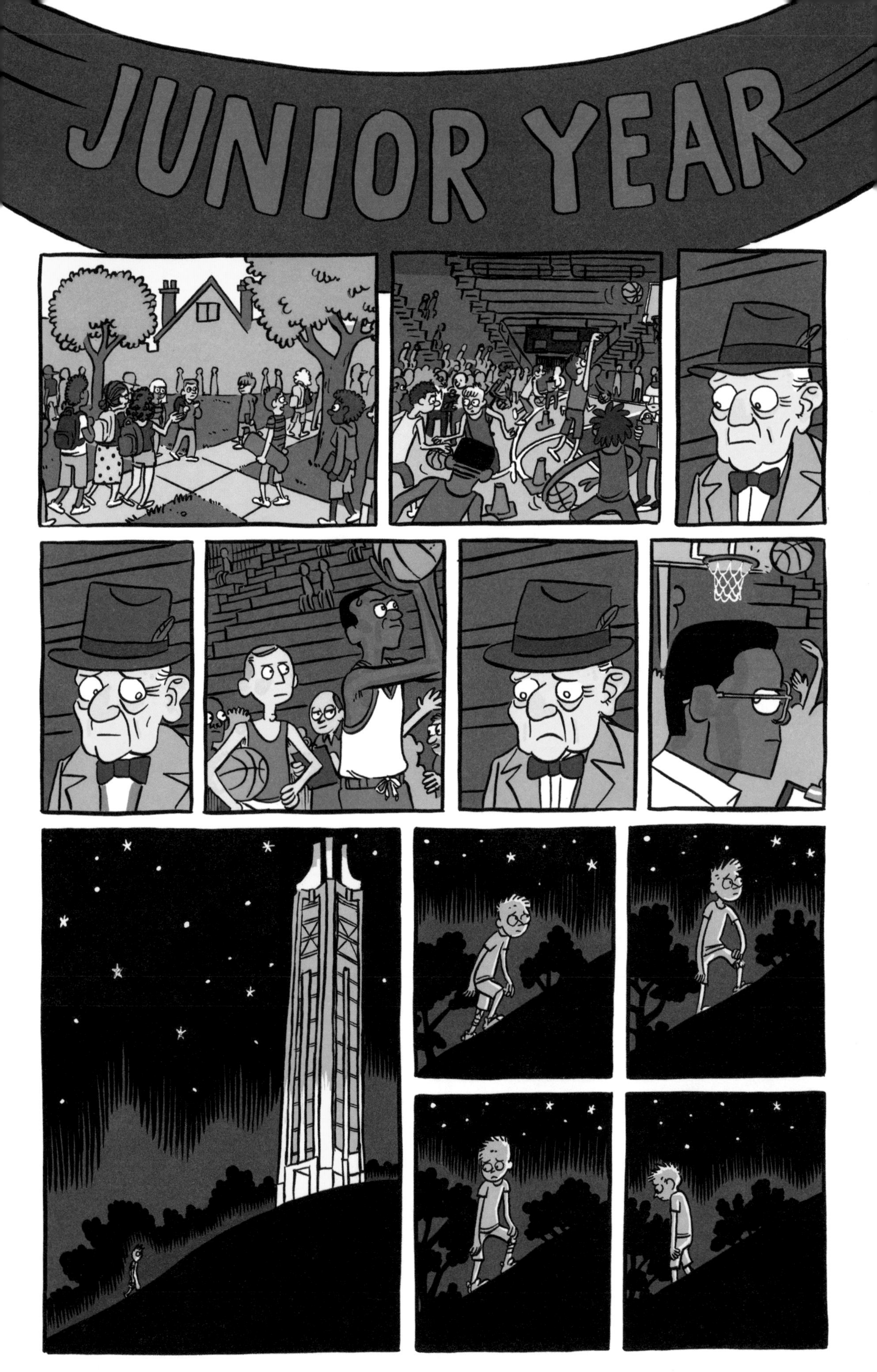
JUNIOR YEAR

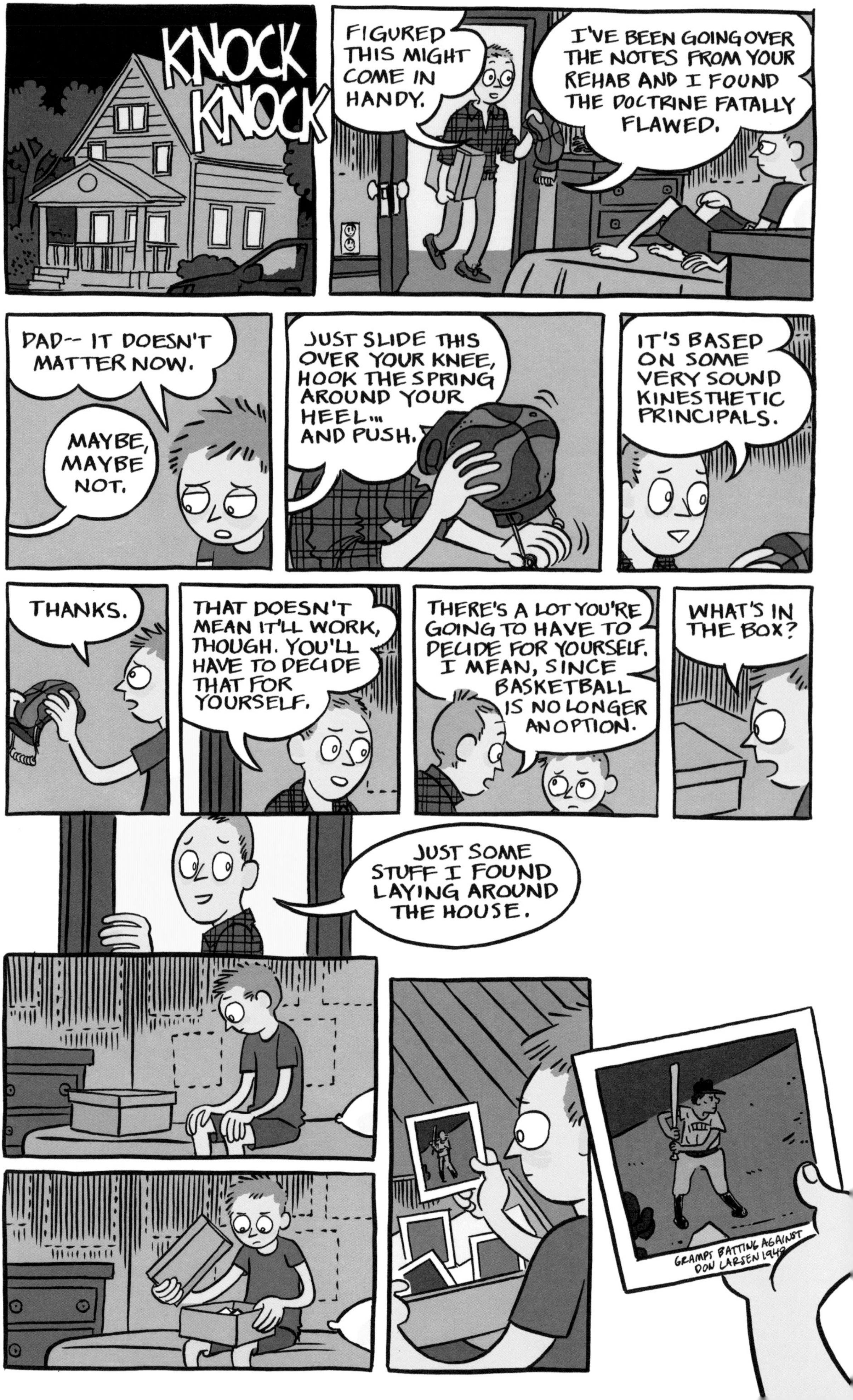

KNOCK KNOCK
FIGURED THIS MIGHT COME IN HANDY.
I'VE BEEN GOING OVER THE NOTES FROM YOUR REHAB AND I FOUND THE DOCTRINE FATALLY FLAWED.
DAD-- IT DOESN'T MATTER NOW.
MAYBE, MAYBE NOT.
JUST SLIDE THIS OVER YOUR KNEE, HOOK THE SPRING AROUND YOUR HEEL... AND PUSH.
IT'S BASED ON SOME VERY SOUND KINESTHETIC PRINCIPALS.
THANKS.
THAT DOESN'T MEAN IT'LL WORK, THOUGH. YOU'LL HAVE TO DECIDE THAT FOR YOURSELF.
THERE'S A LOT YOU'RE GOING TO HAVE TO DECIDE FOR YOURSELF. I MEAN, SINCE BASKETBALL IS NO LONGER AN OPTION.
WHAT'S IN THE BOX?
JUST SOME STUFF I FOUND LAYING AROUND THE HOUSE.
GRAMPS BATTING AGAINST DON LARSEN 1948

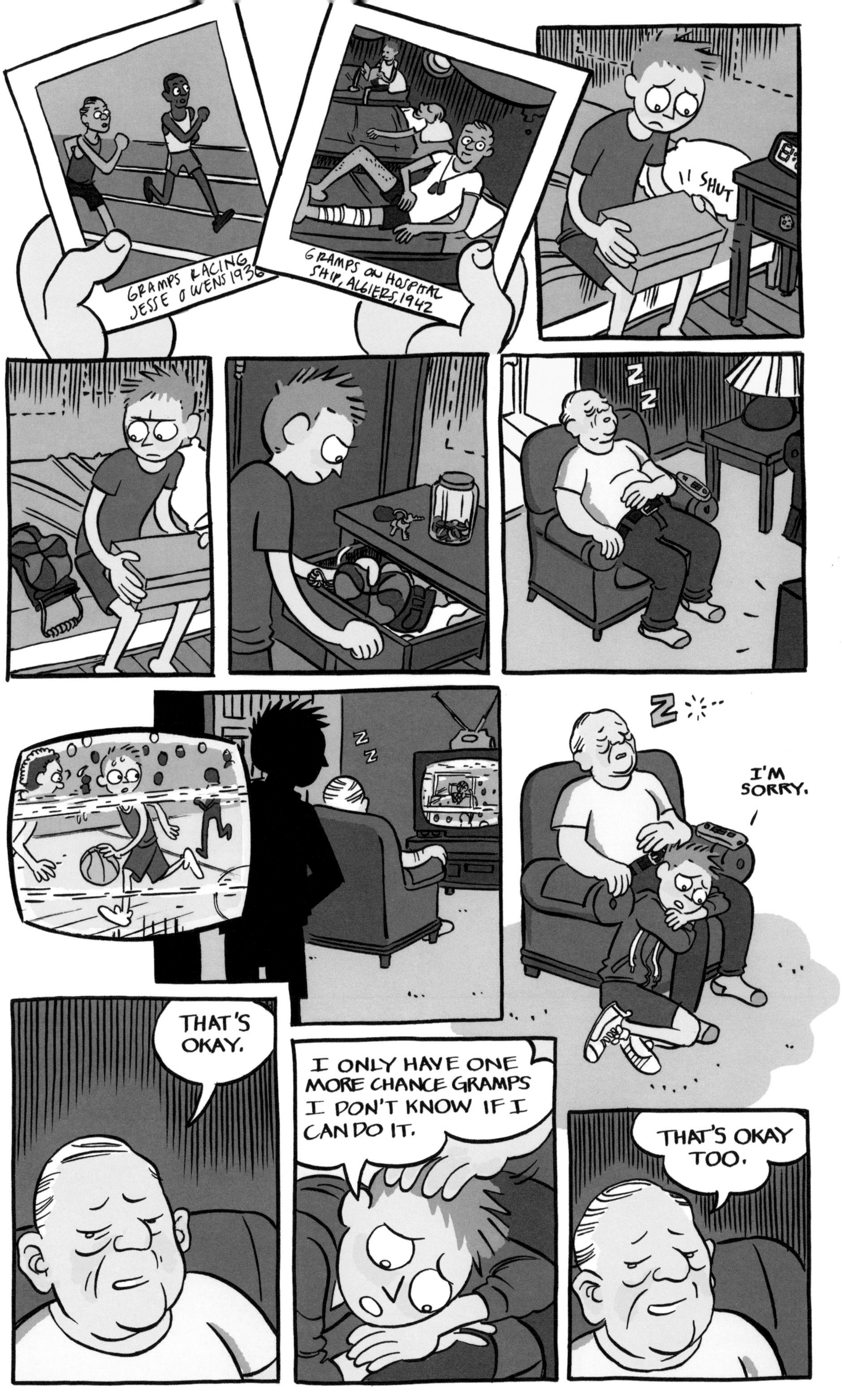
GRAMPS RACING JESSE OWENS 1936
GRAMPS ON HOSPITAL SHIP, ALGIERS, 1942
SHUT
Z Z
Z Z
Z
I'M SORRY.
THAT'S OKAY.
I ONLY HAVE ONE MORE CHANCE GRAMPS I DON'T KNOW IF I CAN DO IT.
THAT'S OKAY TOO.

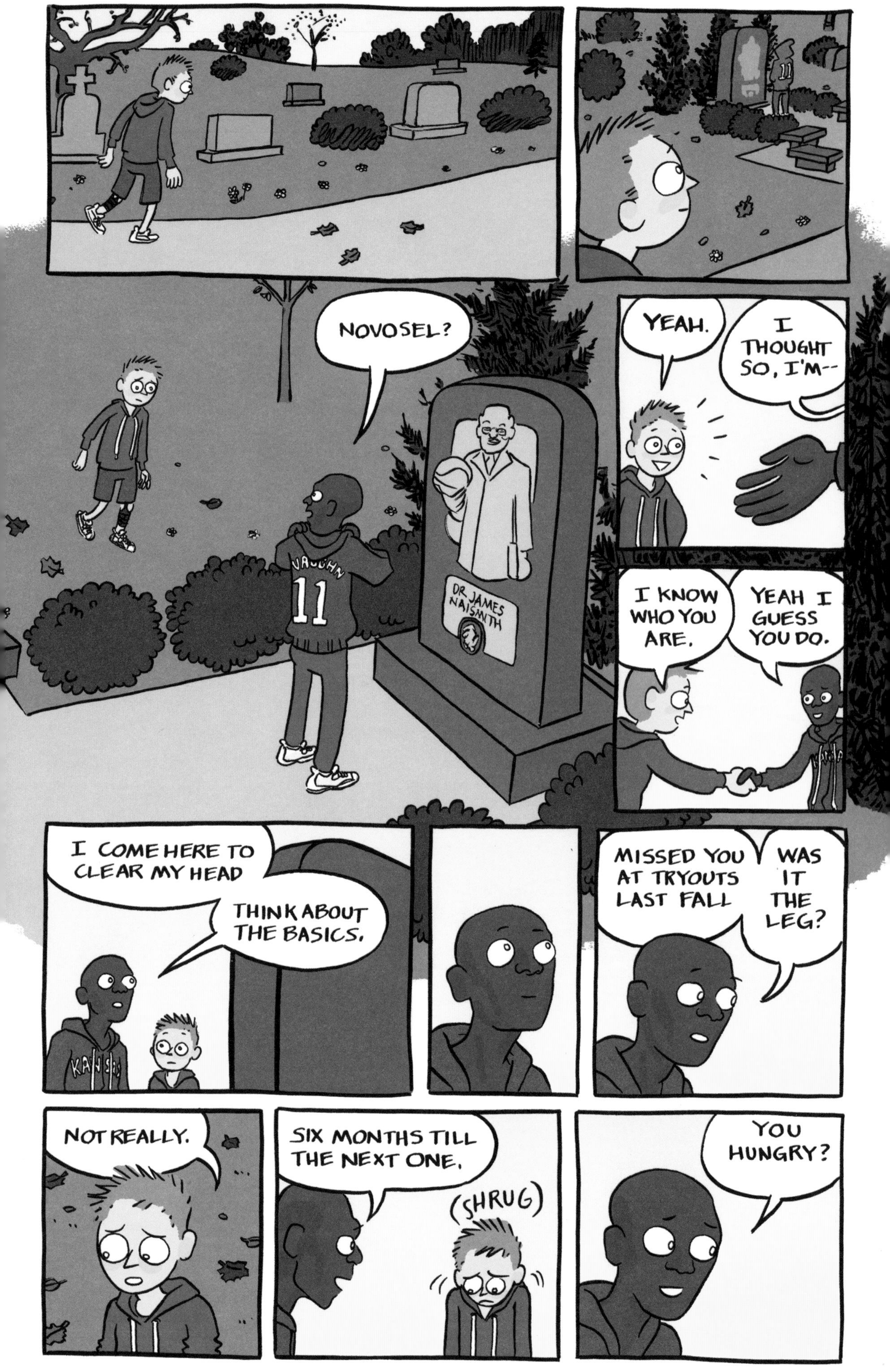
NOVOSEL?
DR JAMES NAISMITH
VAUGHN
11
YEAH.
I THOUGHT SO, I'M--
I KNOW WHO YOU ARE.
YEAH I GUESS YOU DO.
I COME HERE TO CLEAR MY HEAD
THINK ABOUT THE BASICS.
MISSED YOU AT TRYOUTS LAST FALL
WAS IT THE LEG?
NOT REALLY.
SIX MONTHS TILL THE NEXT ONE.
(SHRUG)
YOU HUNGRY?

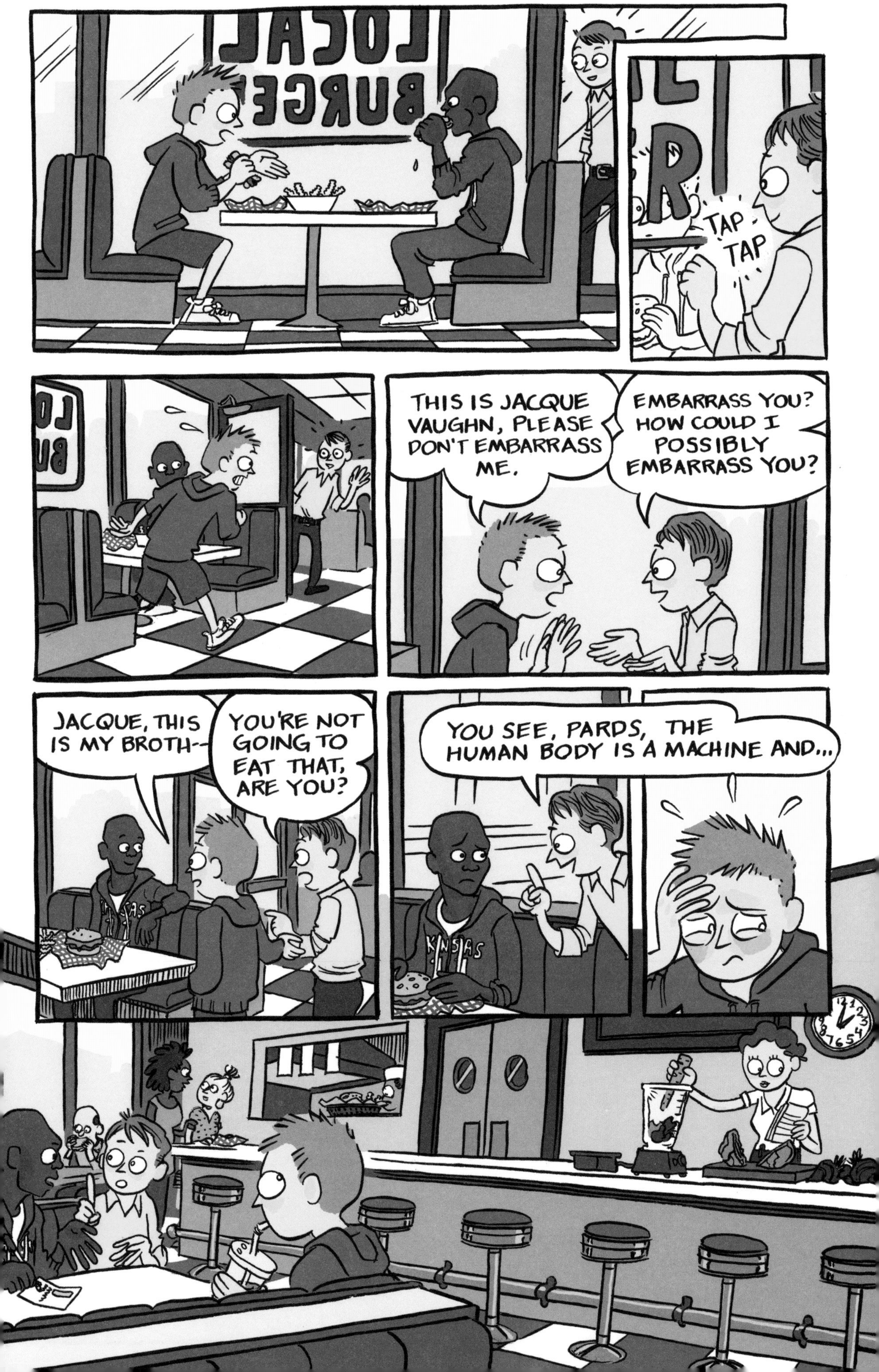
LOCAL
BURGE
TAP
TAP
THIS IS JACQUE VAUGHN, PLEASE DON'T EMBARRASS ME.
EMBARRASS YOU? HOW COULD I POSSIBLY EMBARRASS YOU?
JACQUE, THIS IS MY BROTH--
YOU'RE NOT GOING TO EAT THAT, ARE YOU?
YOU SEE, PARDS, THE HUMAN BODY IS A MACHINE AND...

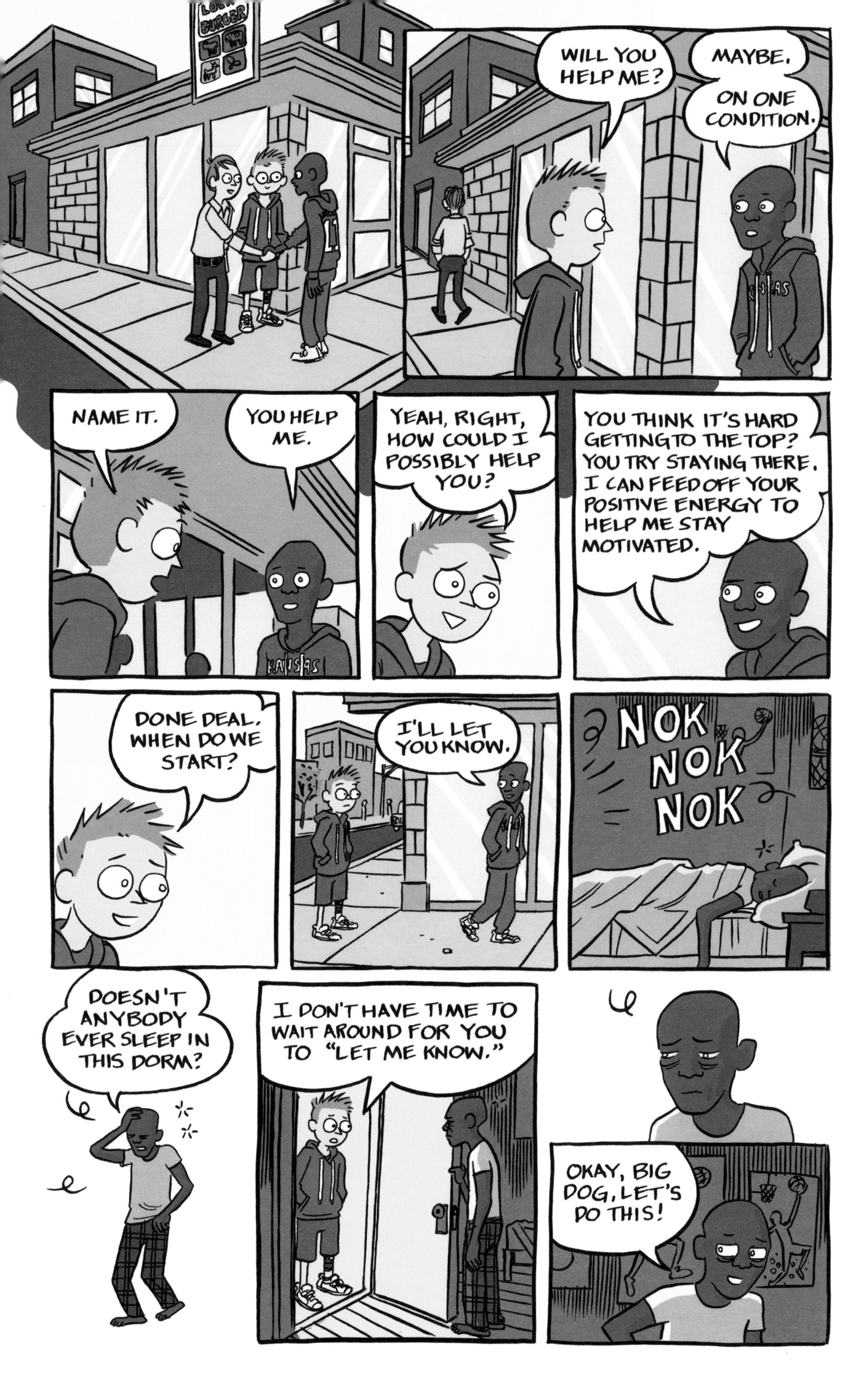
WILL YOU HELP ME?
MAYBE.
ON ONE CONDITION.
NAME IT.
YOU HELP ME.
YEAH, RIGHT, HOW COULD I POSSIBLY HELP YOU?
YOU THINK IT'S HARD GETTING TO THE TOP? YOU TRY STAYING THERE. I CAN FEED OFF YOUR POSITIVE ENERGY TO HELP ME STAY MOTIVATED.
DONE DEAL. WHEN DO WE START?
I'LL LET YOU KNOW.
NOK
NOK
NOK
DOESN'T ANYBODY EVER SLEEP IN THIS DORM?
I DON'T HAVE TIME TO WAIT AROUND FOR YOU TO "LET ME KNOW."
OKAY, BIG DOG, LET'S DO THIS!

KNK

ARE WE GONNA PLAY?

LESSON NUMBER ONE— FORGET EVERYTHING YOU KNOW... EVERYTHING YOU THOUGHT YOU KNEW ABOUT BASKETBALL.

NOW RUN.

RUN WHERE?

EVERYWHERE.

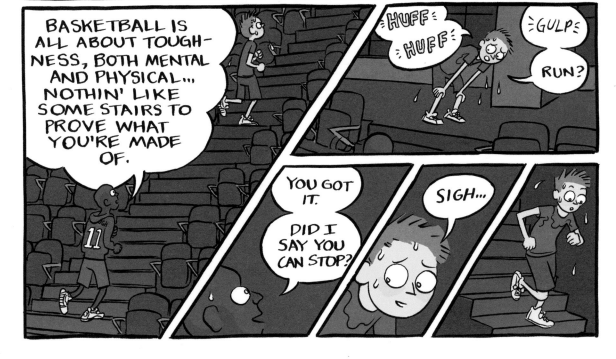

BASKETBALL IS ALL ABOUT TOUGH- NESS, BOTH MENTAL AND PHYSICAL... NOTHIN' LIKE SOME STAIRS TO PROVE WHAT YOU'RE MADE OF.

HUFF HUFF

GULP

RUN?

YOU GOT IT.

DID I SAY YOU CAN STOP?

SIGH...

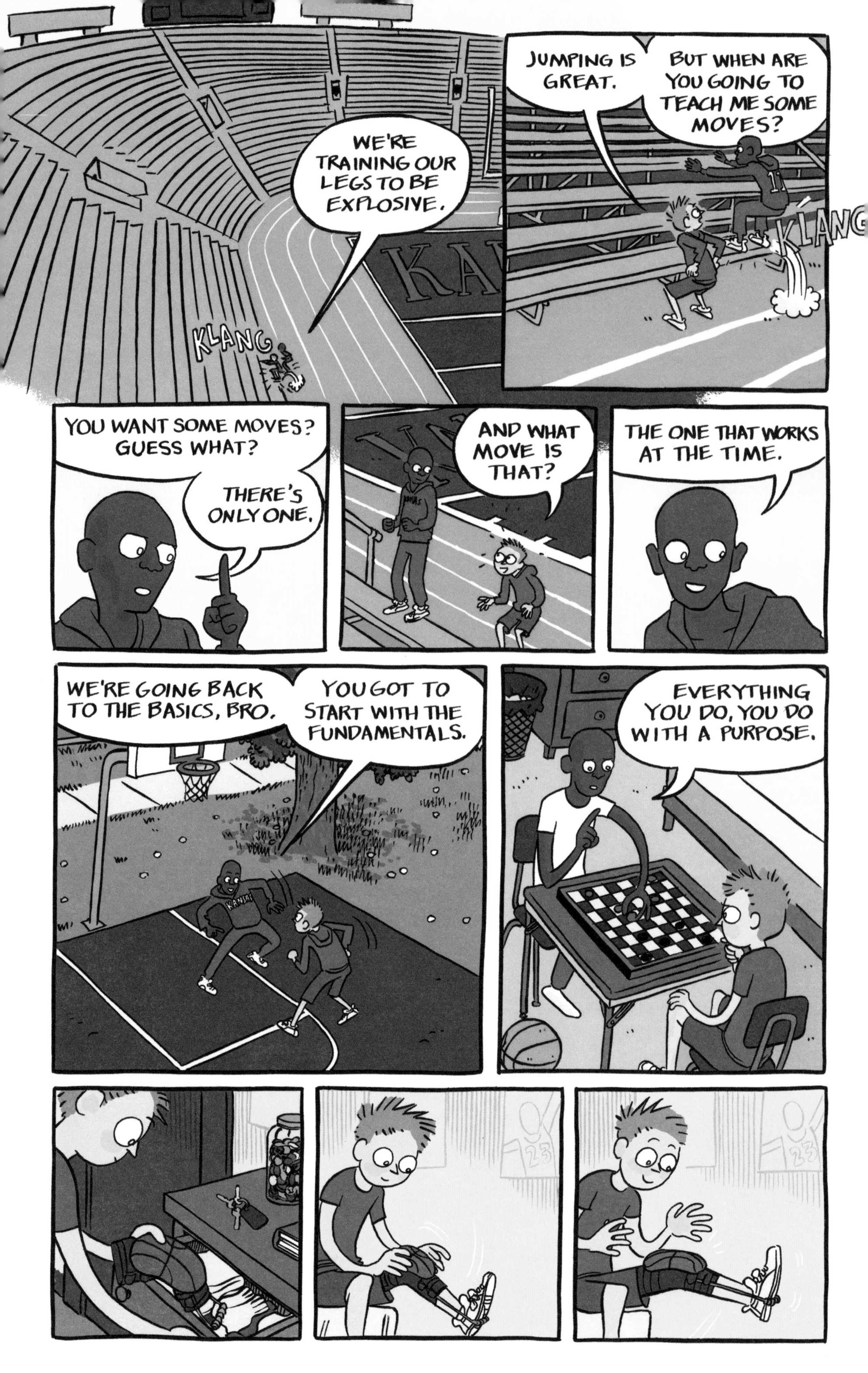
WE'RE TRAINING OUR LEGS TO BE EXPLOSIVE.
KLANG
JUMPING IS GREAT.
BUT WHEN ARE YOU GOING TO TEACH ME SOME MOVES?
KLANG
YOU WANT SOME MOVES? GUESS WHAT?
THERE'S ONLY ONE.
AND WHAT MOVE IS THAT?
THE ONE THAT WORKS AT THE TIME.
WE'RE GOING BACK TO THE BASICS, BRO.
YOU GOT TO START WITH THE FUNDAMENTALS.
EVERYTHING YOU DO, YOU DO WITH A PURPOSE.

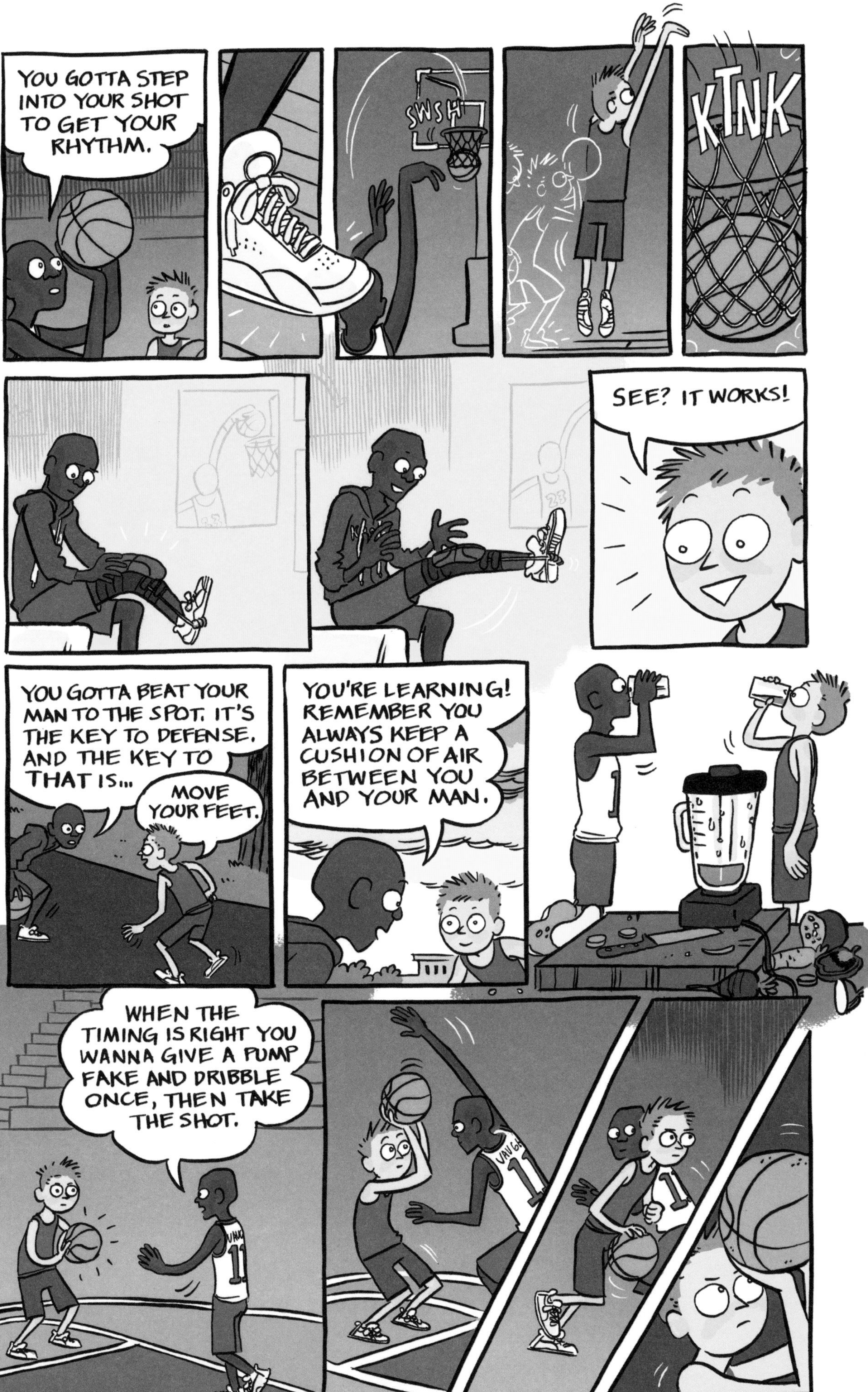
YOU GOTTA STEP INTO YOUR SHOT TO GET YOUR RHYTHM.
SWSH
KTNK
SEE? IT WORKS!
YOU GOTTA BEAT YOUR MAN TO THE SPOT. IT'S THE KEY TO DEFENSE. AND THE KEY TO THAT IS...
MOVE YOUR FEET.
YOU'RE LEARNING! REMEMBER YOU ALWAYS KEEP A CUSHION OF AIR BETWEEN YOU AND YOUR MAN.
WHEN THE TIMING IS RIGHT YOU WANNA GIVE A PUMP FAKE AND DRIBBLE ONCE, THEN TAKE THE SHOT.

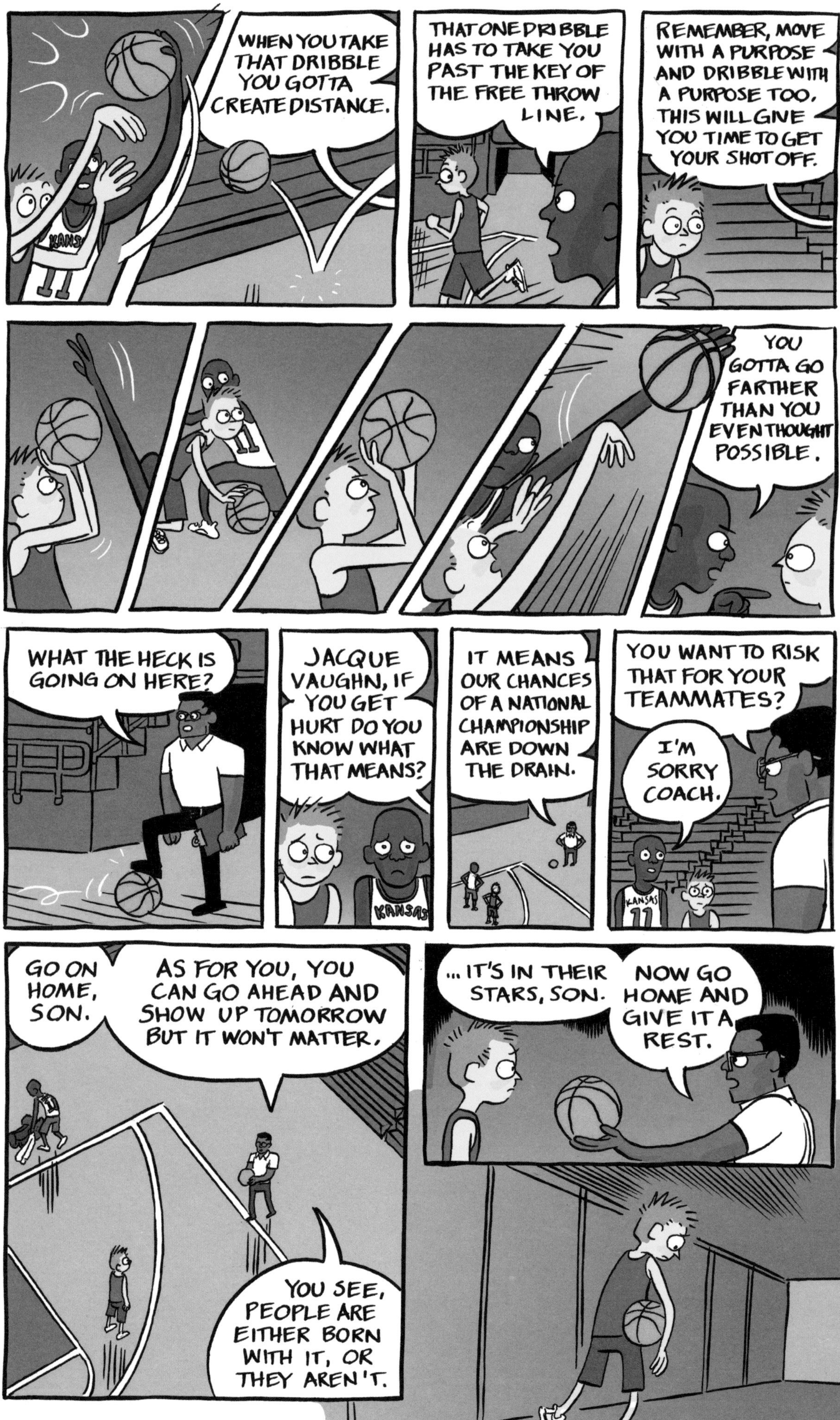
WHEN YOU TAKE THAT DRIBBLE YOU GOTTA CREATE DISTANCE.
THAT ONE DRIBBLE HAS TO TAKE YOU PAST THE KEY OF THE FREE THROW LINE.
REMEMBER, MOVE WITH A PURPOSE AND DRIBBLE WITH A PURPOSE TOO, THIS WILL GIVE YOU TIME TO GET YOUR SHOT OFF.
YOU GOTTA GO FARTHER THAN YOU EVEN THOUGHT POSSIBLE.
WHAT THE HECK IS GOING ON HERE?
JACQUE VAUGHN, IF YOU GET HURT DO YOU KNOW WHAT THAT MEANS?
IT MEANS OUR CHANCES OF A NATIONAL CHAMPIONSHIP ARE DOWN THE DRAIN.
YOU WANT TO RISK THAT FOR YOUR TEAMMATES?
I'M SORRY COACH.
GO ON HOME, SON.
AS FOR YOU, YOU CAN GO AHEAD AND SHOW UP TOMORROW BUT IT WON'T MATTER.
YOU SEE, PEOPLE ARE EITHER BORN WITH IT, OR THEY AREN'T.
... IT'S IN THEIR STARS, SON.
NOW GO HOME AND GIVE IT A REST.

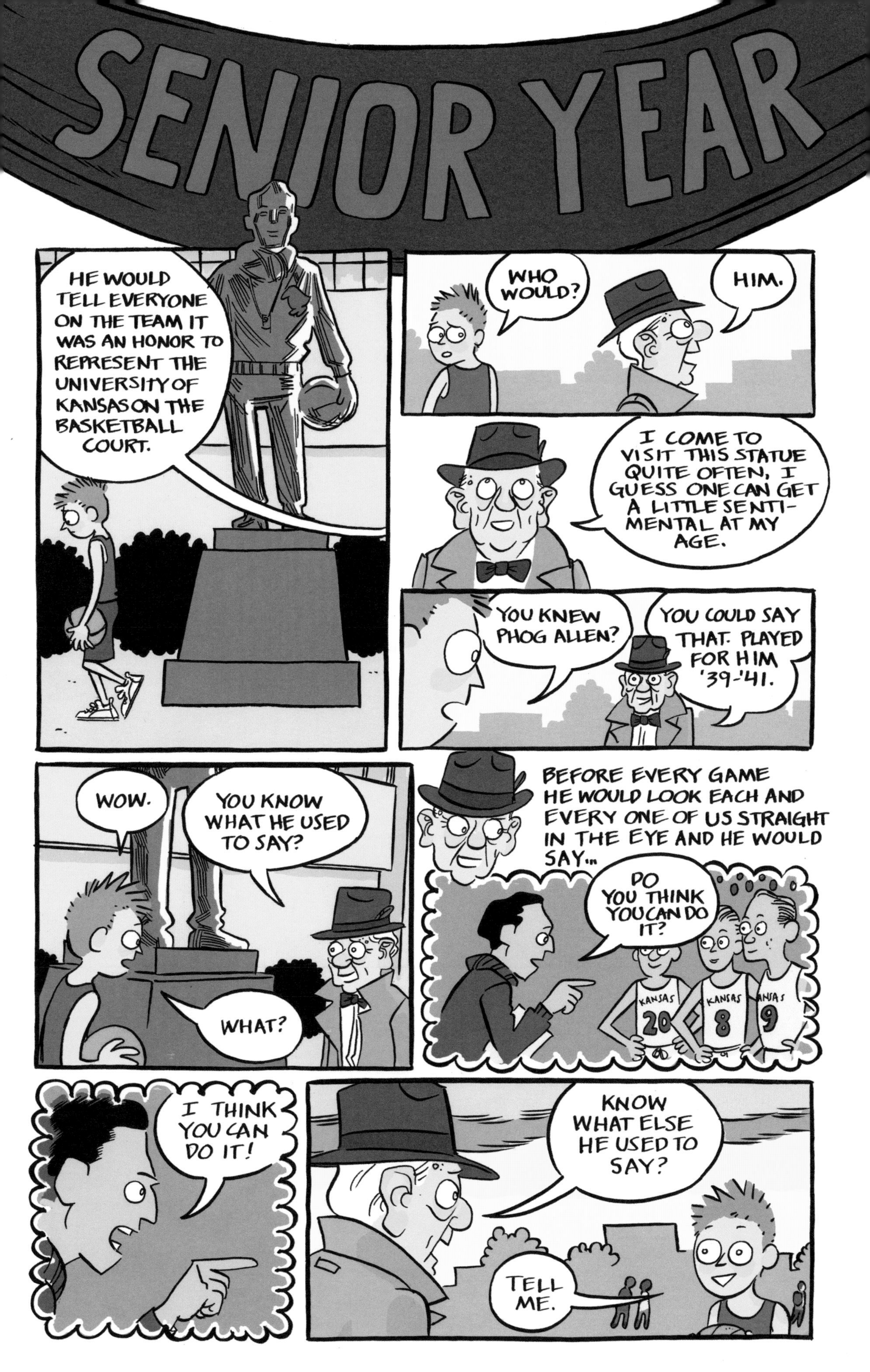
SENIOR YEAR
HE WOULD TELL EVERYONE ON THE TEAM IT WAS AN HONOR TO REPRESENT THE UNIVERSITY OF KANSAS ON THE BASKETBALL COURT.
WHO WOULD?
HIM.
I COME TO VISIT THIS STATUE QUITE OFTEN, I GUESS ONE CAN GET A LITTLE SENTI-MENTAL AT MY AGE.
YOU KNEW PHOG ALLEN?
YOU COULD SAY THAT. PLAYED FOR HIM '39-'41.
WOW.
YOU KNOW WHAT HE USED TO SAY?
WHAT?
BEFORE EVERY GAME HE WOULD LOOK EACH AND EVERY ONE OF US STRAIGHT IN THE EYE AND HE WOULD SAY...
DO YOU THINK YOU CAN DO IT?
KANSAS 20
KANSAS 8
KANSAS 9
I THINK YOU CAN DO IT!
KNOW WHAT ELSE HE USED TO SAY?
TELL ME.

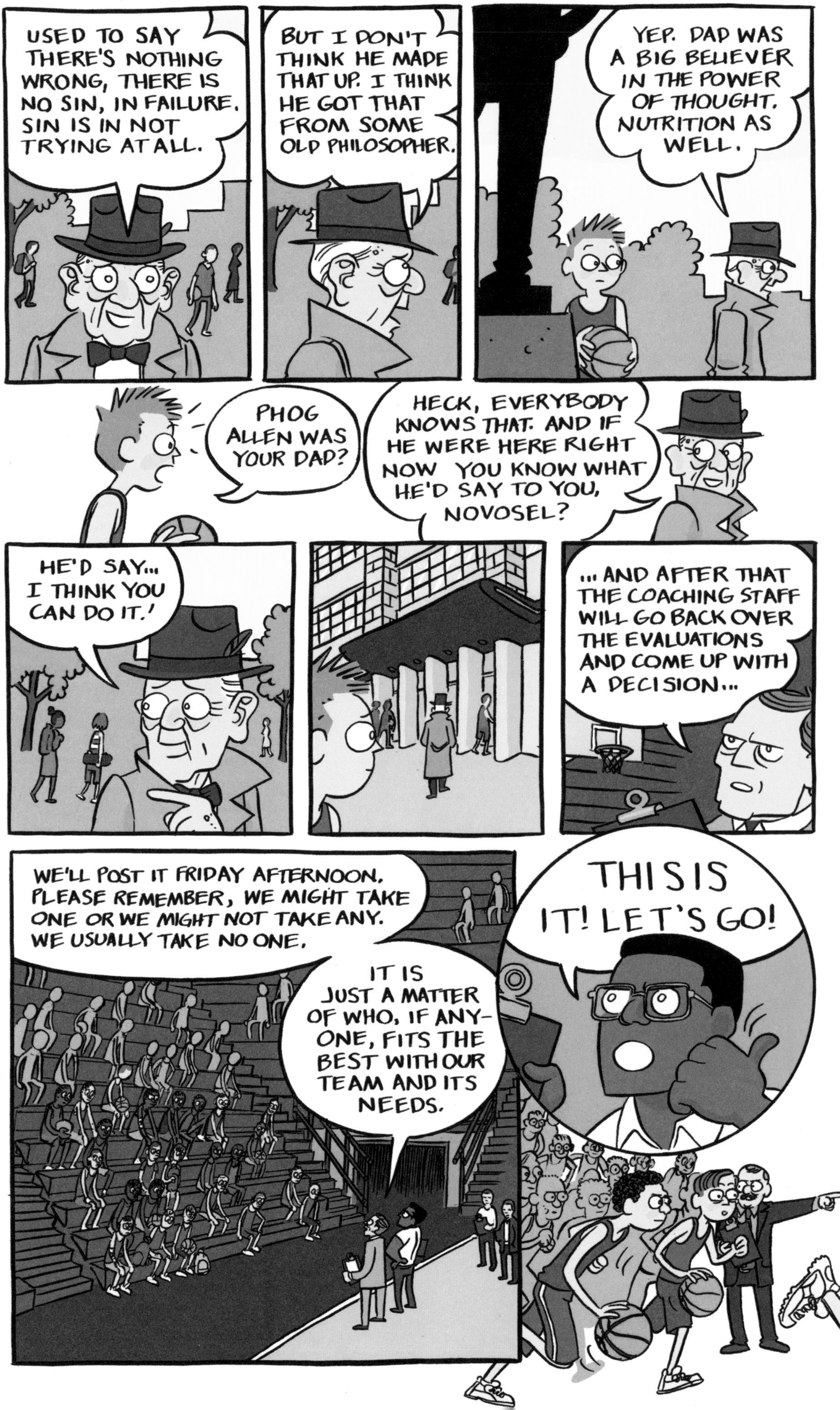
USED TO SAY THERE'S NOTHING WRONG, THERE IS NO SIN, IN FAILURE. SIN IS IN NOT TRYING AT ALL.
BUT I DON'T THINK HE MADE THAT UP. I THINK HE GOT THAT FROM SOME OLD PHILOSOPHER.
YEP. DAD WAS A BIG BELIEVER IN THE POWER OF THOUGHT. NUTRITION AS WELL.
PHOG ALLEN WAS YOUR DAD?
HECK, EVERYBODY KNOWS THAT. AND IF HE WERE HERE RIGHT NOW YOU KNOW WHAT HE'D SAY TO YOU, NOVOSEL?
HE'D SAY... I THINK YOU CAN DO IT.'
...AND AFTER THAT THE COACHING STAFF WILL GO BACK OVER THE EVALUATIONS AND COME UP WITH A DECISION...
WE'LL POST IT FRIDAY AFTERNOON. PLEASE REMEMBER, WE MIGHT TAKE ONE OR WE MIGHT NOT TAKE ANY. WE USUALLY TAKE NO ONE.
IT IS JUST A MATTER OF WHO, IF ANY-ONE, FITS THE BEST WITH OUR TEAM AND ITS NEEDS.
THIS IS IT! LET'S GO!

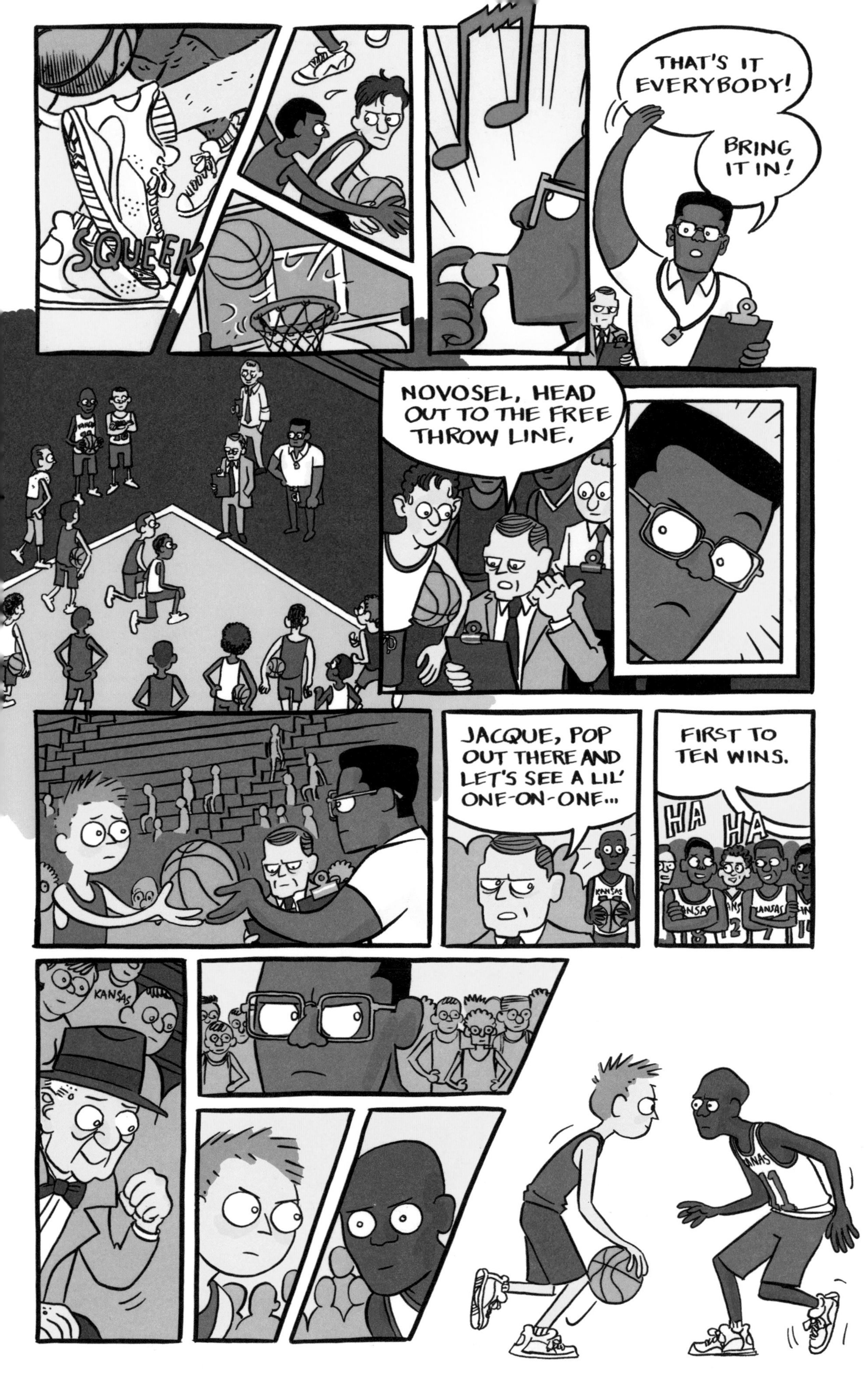
SQUEEK
THAT'S IT EVERYBODY!
BRING IT IN!
NOVOSEL, HEAD OUT TO THE FREE THROW LINE,
JACQUE, POP OUT THERE AND LET'S SEE A LIL' ONE-ON-ONE...
FIRST TO TEN WINS.
HA
HA
KANSAS

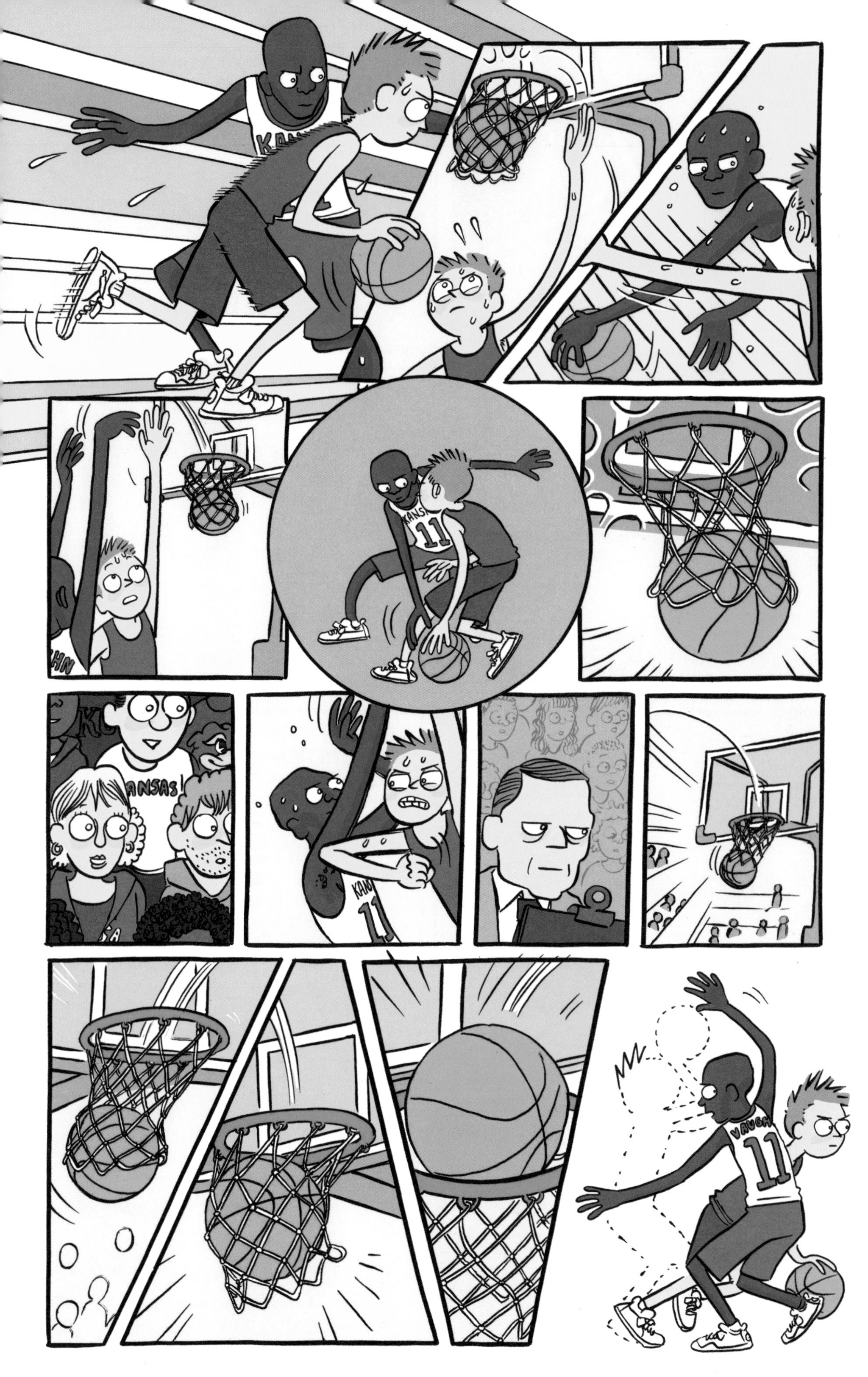

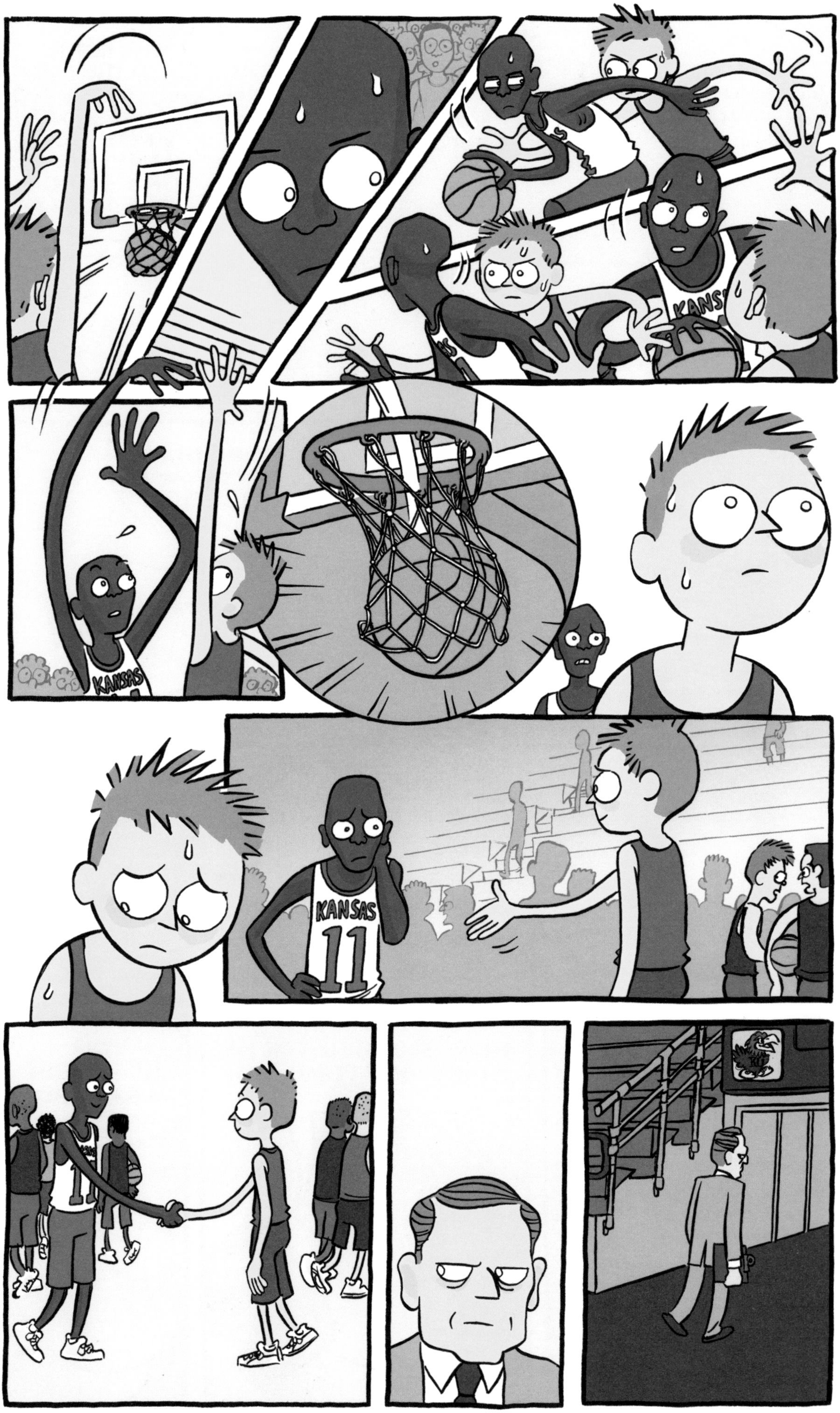
KANSAS
11

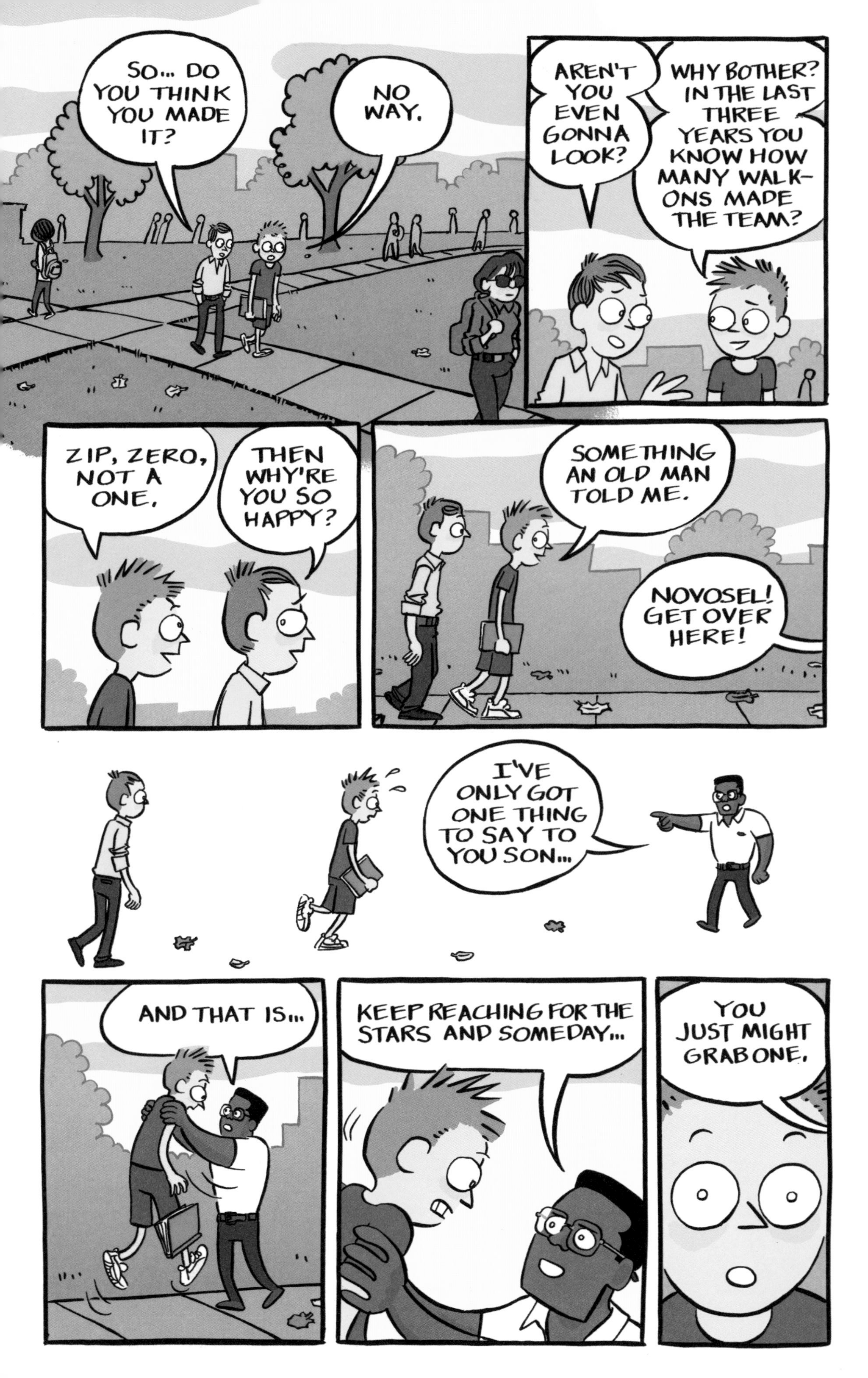
SO... DO YOU THINK YOU MADE IT?
NO WAY.
AREN'T YOU EVEN GONNA LOOK?
WHY BOTHER? IN THE LAST THREE YEARS YOU KNOW HOW MANY WALK-ONS MADE THE TEAM?
ZIP, ZERO, NOT A ONE.
THEN WHY'RE YOU SO HAPPY?
SOMETHING AN OLD MAN TOLD ME.
NOVOSEL! GET OVER HERE!
I'VE ONLY GOT ONE THING TO SAY TO YOU SON...
AND THAT IS...
KEEP REACHING FOR THE STARS AND SOMEDAY...
YOU JUST MIGHT GRAB ONE.

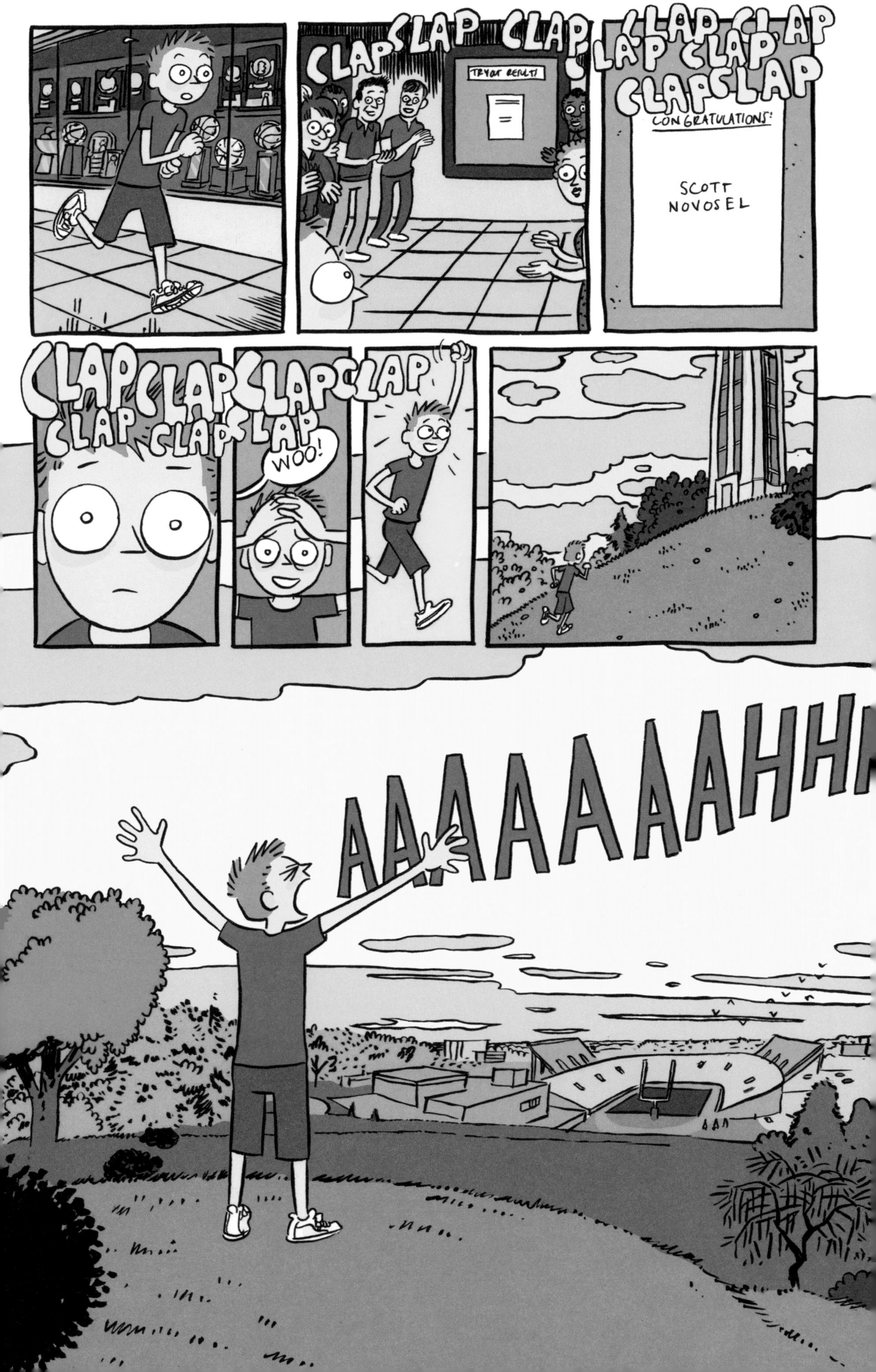
CLAP CLAP CLAP CLAP CLAP CLAP CLAP CLAP CLAP
TRYOUT RESULTS
CONGRATULATIONS!
SCOTT NOVOSEL
CLAP CLAP CLAP CLAP CLAP CLAP CLAP
WOO!
AAAAAAAHH

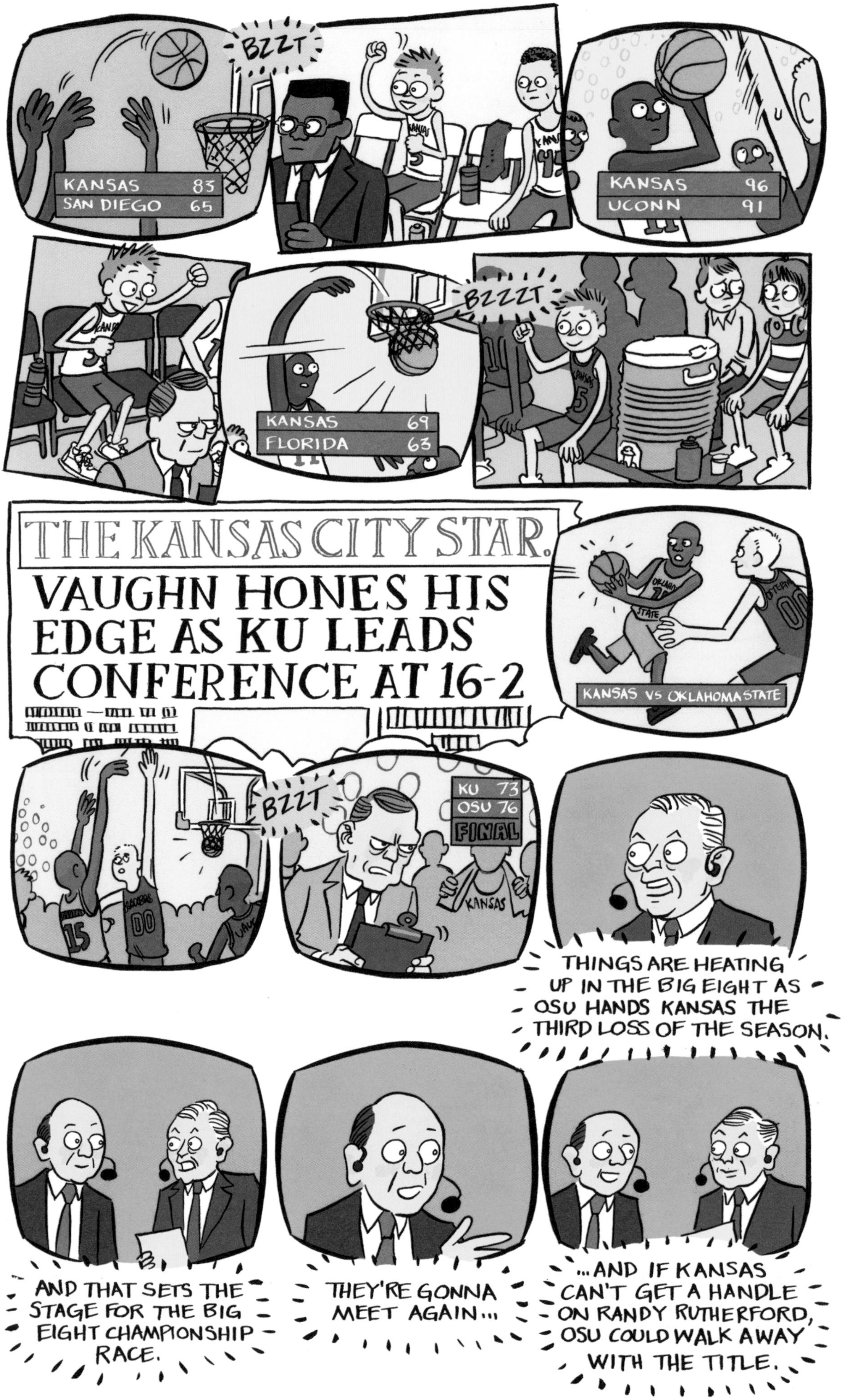

KANSAS 83
SAN DIEGO 65
BZZT
KANSAS
KANSAS 96
UCONN 91
KANSAS 69
FLORIDA 63
BZZZT
THE KANSAS CITY STAR.
VAUGHN HONES HIS EDGE AS KU LEADS CONFERENCE AT 16-2
KANSAS VS OKLAHOMA STATE
BZZT
KU 73
OSU 76
FINAL
KANSAS
THINGS ARE HEATING UP IN THE BIG EIGHT AS OSU HANDS KANSAS THE THIRD LOSS OF THE SEASON.
AND THAT SETS THE STAGE FOR THE BIG EIGHT CHAMPIONSHIP RACE.
THEY'RE GONNA MEET AGAIN...
...AND IF KANSAS CAN'T GET A HANDLE ON RANDY RUTHERFORD, OSU COULD WALK AWAY WITH THE TITLE.

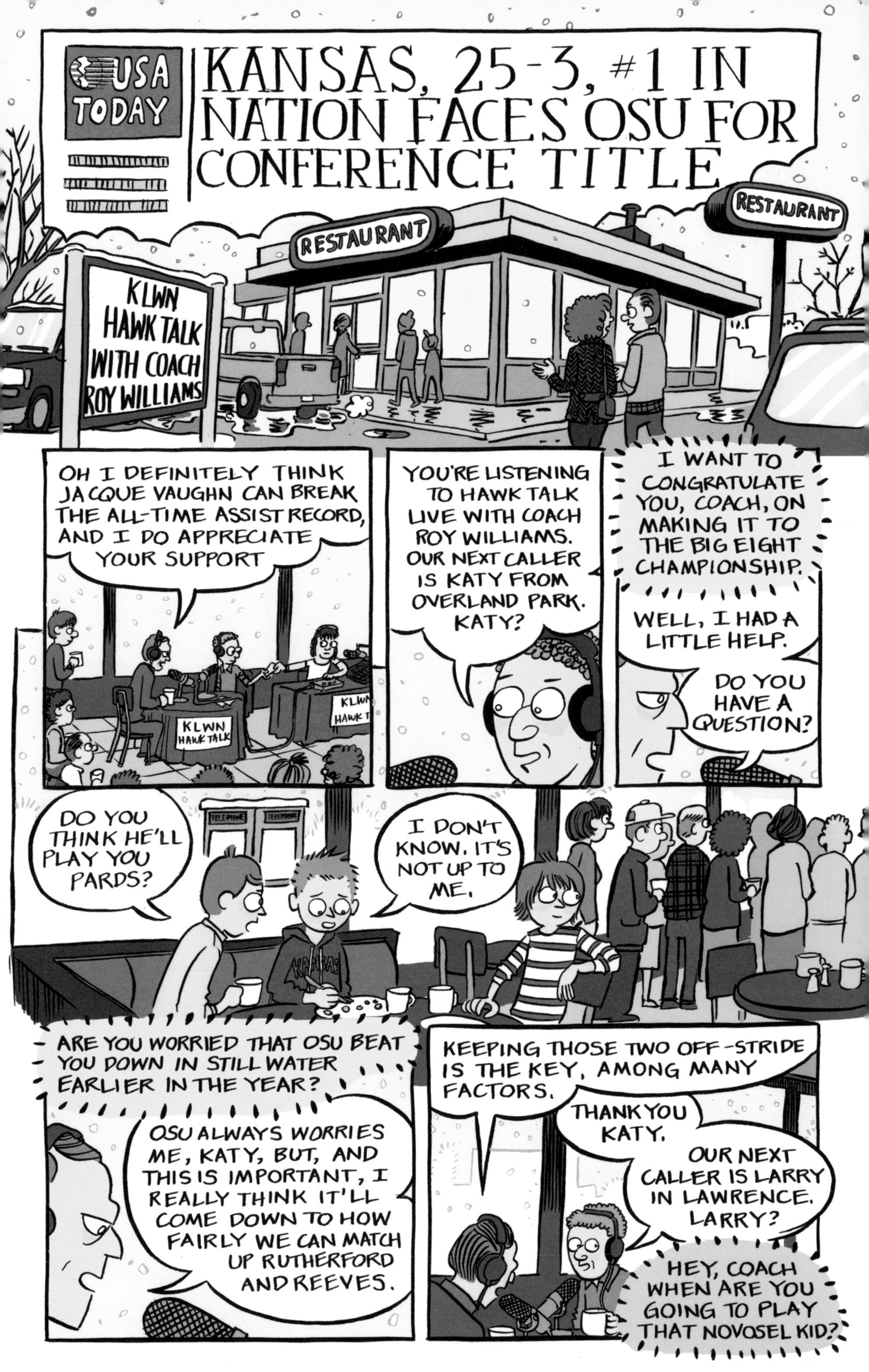
USA TODAY
KANSAS, 25-3, #1 IN NATION FACES OSU FOR CONFERENCE TITLE
RESTAURANT
RESTAURANT
KLWN HAWK TALK WITH COACH ROY WILLIAMS
OH I DEFINITELY THINK JACQUE VAUGHN CAN BREAK THE ALL-TIME ASSIST RECORD, AND I DO APPRECIATE YOUR SUPPORT
KLWN HAWK TALK
YOU'RE LISTENING TO HAWK TALK LIVE WITH COACH ROY WILLIAMS. OUR NEXT CALLER IS KATY FROM OVERLAND PARK. KATY?
I WANT TO CONGRATULATE YOU, COACH, ON MAKING IT TO THE BIG EIGHT CHAMPIONSHIP.
WELL, I HAD A LITTLE HELP.
DO YOU HAVE A QUESTION?
DO YOU THINK HE'LL PLAY YOU PARDS?
I DON'T KNOW. IT'S NOT UP TO ME.
KANSAS
ARE YOU WORRIED THAT OSU BEAT YOU DOWN IN STILL WATER EARLIER IN THE YEAR?
OSU ALWAYS WORRIES ME, KATY, BUT, AND THIS IS IMPORTANT, I REALLY THINK IT'LL COME DOWN TO HOW FAIRLY WE CAN MATCH UP RUTHERFORD AND REEVES.
KEEPING THOSE TWO OFF-STRIDE IS THE KEY, AMONG MANY FACTORS.
THANK YOU KATY.
OUR NEXT CALLER IS LARRY IN LAWRENCE. LARRY?
HEY, COACH WHEN ARE YOU GOING TO PLAY THAT NOVOSEL KID?

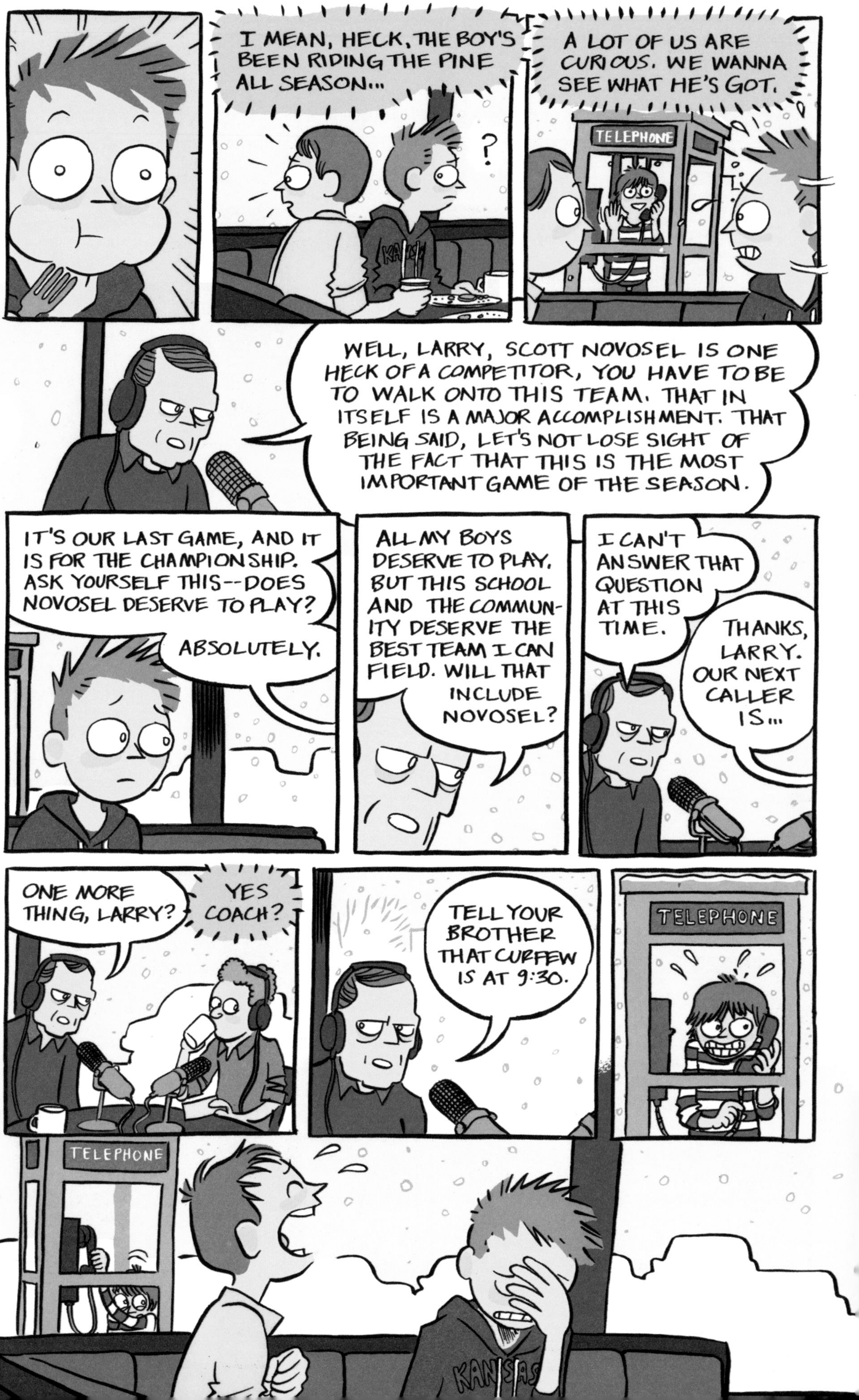
I MEAN, HECK, THE BOY'S BEEN RIDING THE PINE ALL SEASON...
A LOT OF US ARE CURIOUS. WE WANNA SEE WHAT HE'S GOT.
?
TELEPHONE
WELL, LARRY, SCOTT NOVOSEL IS ONE HECK OF A COMPETITOR, YOU HAVE TO BE TO WALK ONTO THIS TEAM. THAT IN ITSELF IS A MAJOR ACCOMPLISHMENT. THAT BEING SAID, LET'S NOT LOSE SIGHT OF THE FACT THAT THIS IS THE MOST IMPORTANT GAME OF THE SEASON.
IT'S OUR LAST GAME, AND IT IS FOR THE CHAMPIONSHIP. ASK YOURSELF THIS--DOES NOVOSEL DESERVE TO PLAY?
ABSOLUTELY.
ALL MY BOYS DESERVE TO PLAY. BUT THIS SCHOOL AND THE COMMUNITY DESERVE THE BEST TEAM I CAN FIELD. WILL THAT INCLUDE NOVOSEL?
I CAN'T ANSWER THAT QUESTION AT THIS TIME.
THANKS, LARRY. OUR NEXT CALLER IS...
ONE MORE THING, LARRY?
YES COACH?
TELL YOUR BROTHER THAT CURFEW IS AT 9:30.
TELEPHONE
TELEPHONE
KANSAS

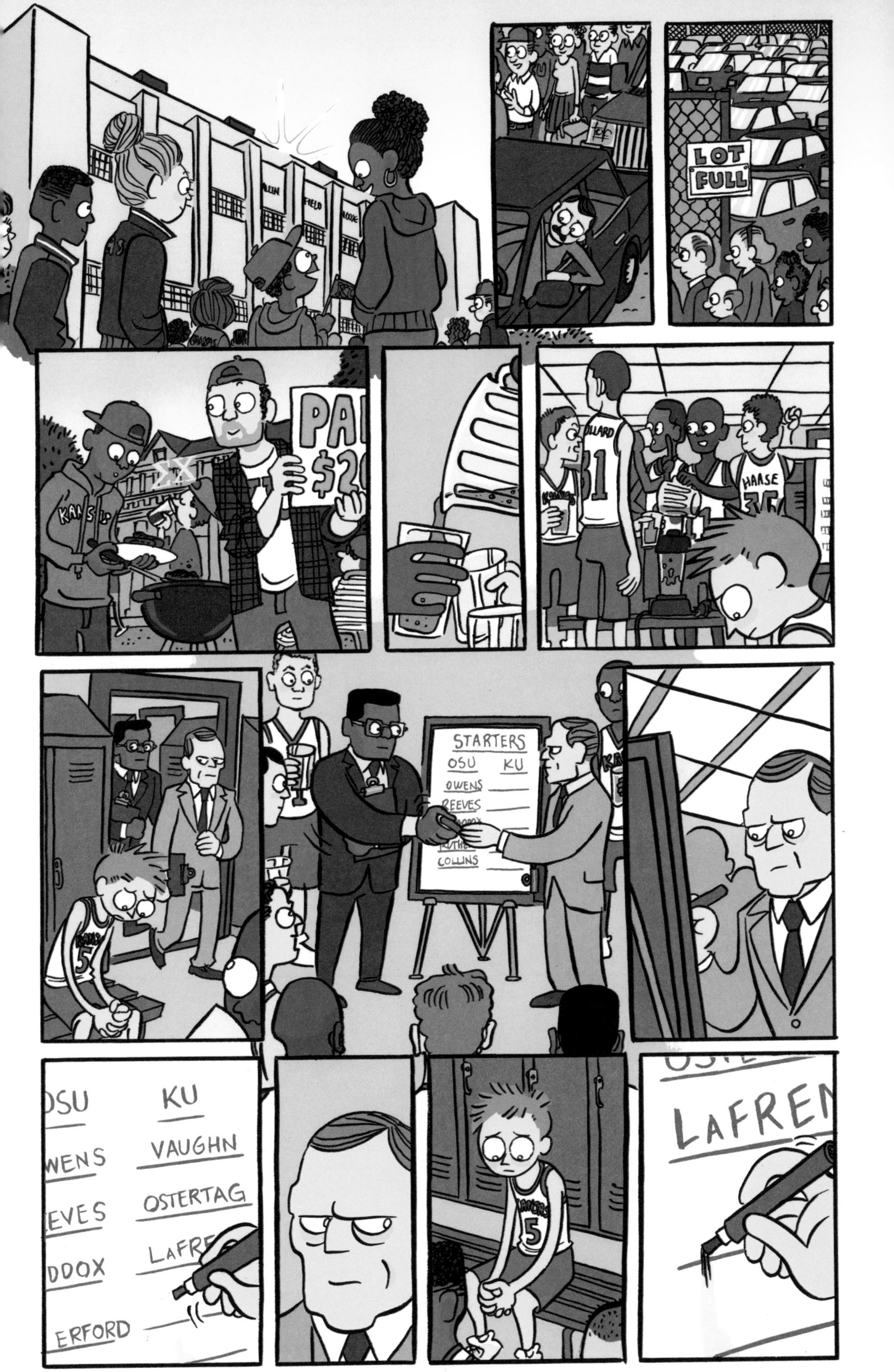
LOT FULL
PA
$20
ΣX
HAASE
35
STARTERS
OSU
KU
OWENS
REEVES
COLLINS
OSU
KU
WENS
VAUGHN
EVES
OSTERTAG
DDOX
LaFRE
ERFORD
5
LaFREN

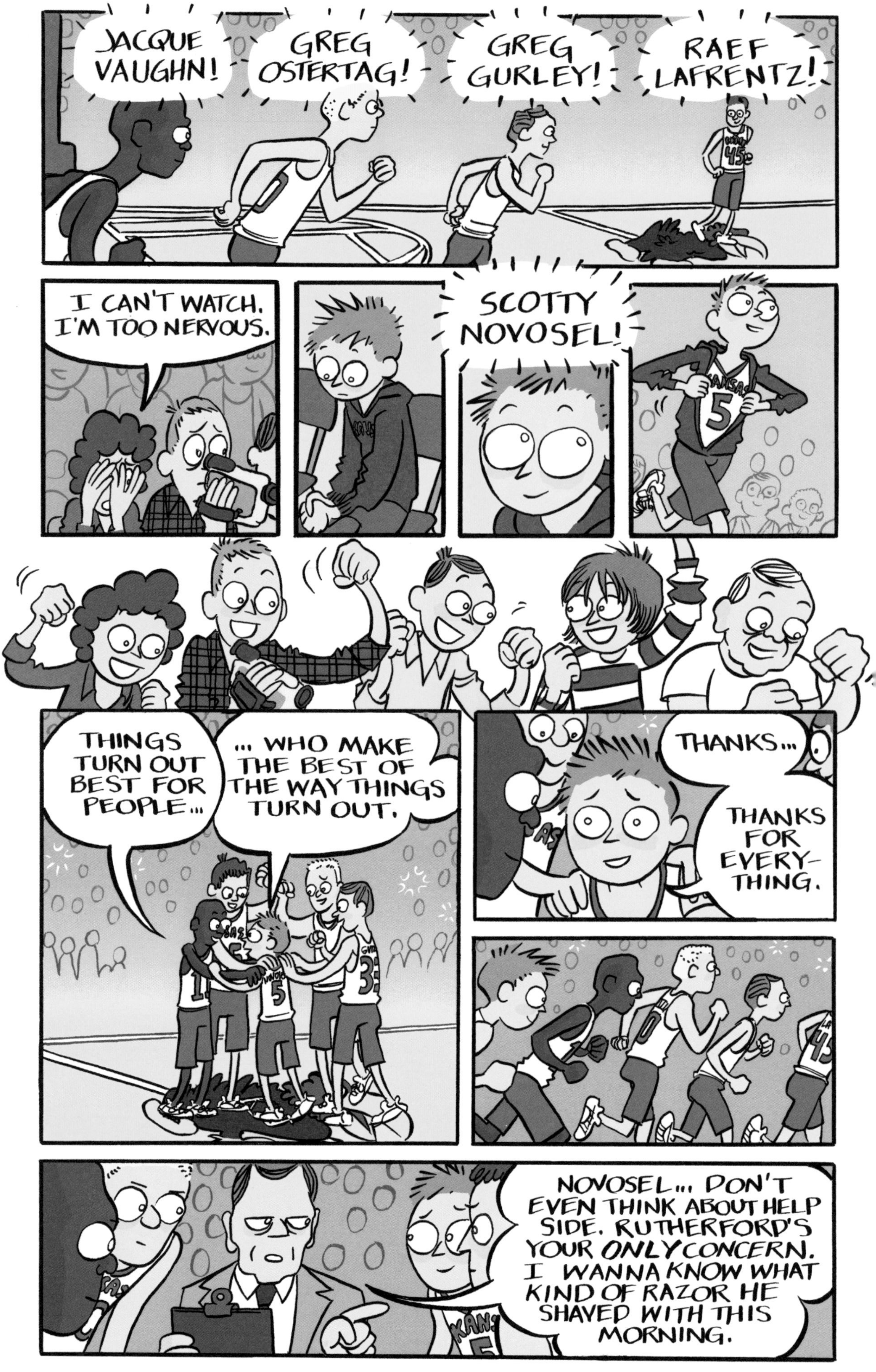
JACQUE VAUGHN!
GREG OSTERTAG!
GREG GURLEY!
RAEF LAFRENTZ!
I CAN'T WATCH. I'M TOO NERVOUS.
SCOTTY NOVOSEL!
THINGS TURN OUT BEST FOR PEOPLE...
... WHO MAKE THE BEST OF THE WAY THINGS TURN OUT.
THANKS...
THANKS FOR EVERY-THING.
NOVOSEL... DON'T EVEN THINK ABOUT HELP SIDE. RUTHERFORD'S YOUR ONLY CONCERN. I WANNA KNOW WHAT KIND OF RAZOR HE SHAVED WITH THIS MORNING.

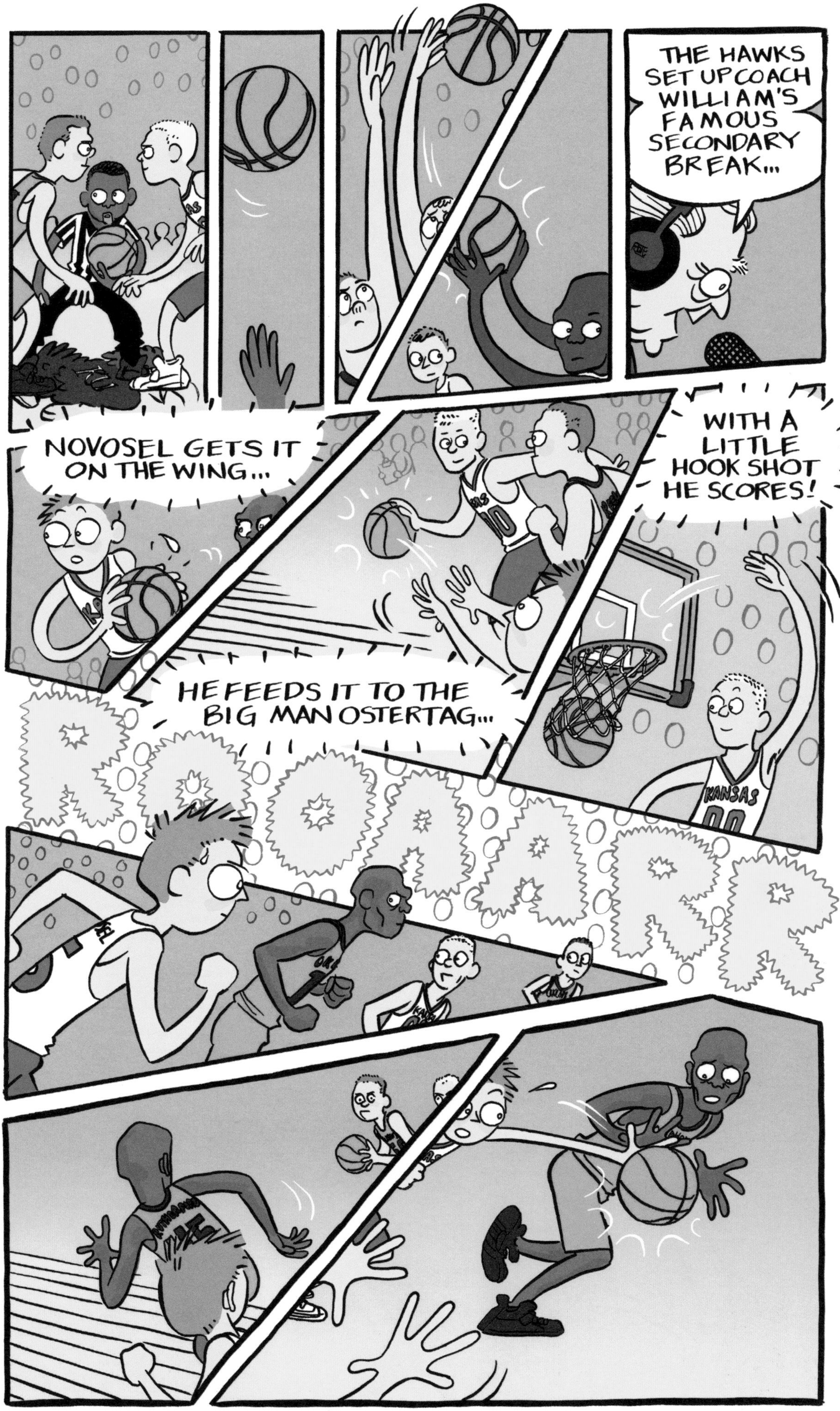
THE HAWKS SET UP COACH WILLIAM'S FAMOUS SECONDARY BREAK...
NOVOSEL GETS IT ON THE WING...
HE FEEDS IT TO THE BIG MAN OSTERTAG...
WITH A LITTLE HOOK SHOT HE SCORES!
RROOAARR
KANSAS 00

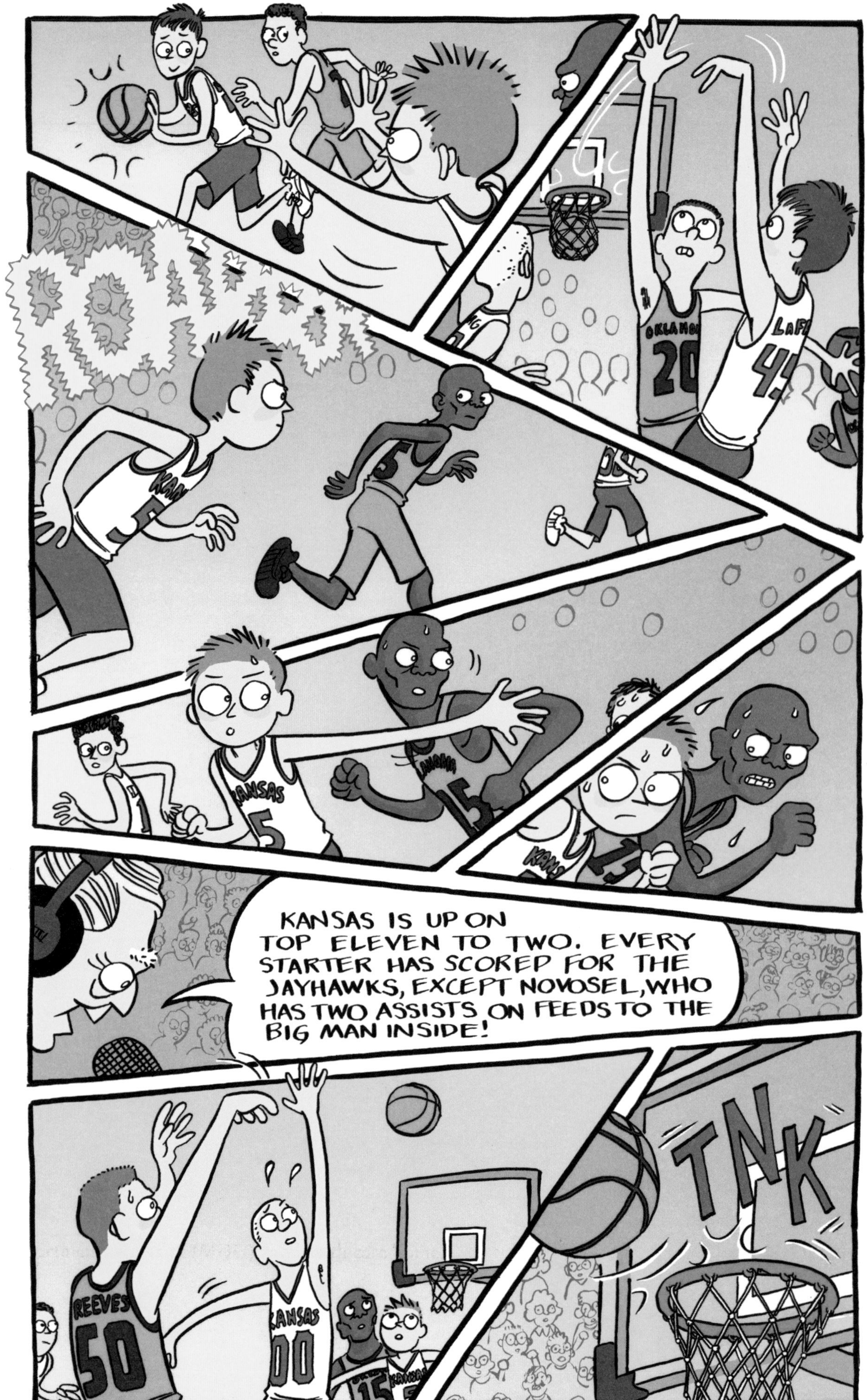
KANSAS IS UP ON TOP ELEVEN TO TWO. EVERY STARTER HAS SCORED FOR THE JAYHAWKS, EXCEPT NOVOSEL, WHO HAS TWO ASSISTS ON FEEDS TO THE BIG MAN INSIDE!
TNK

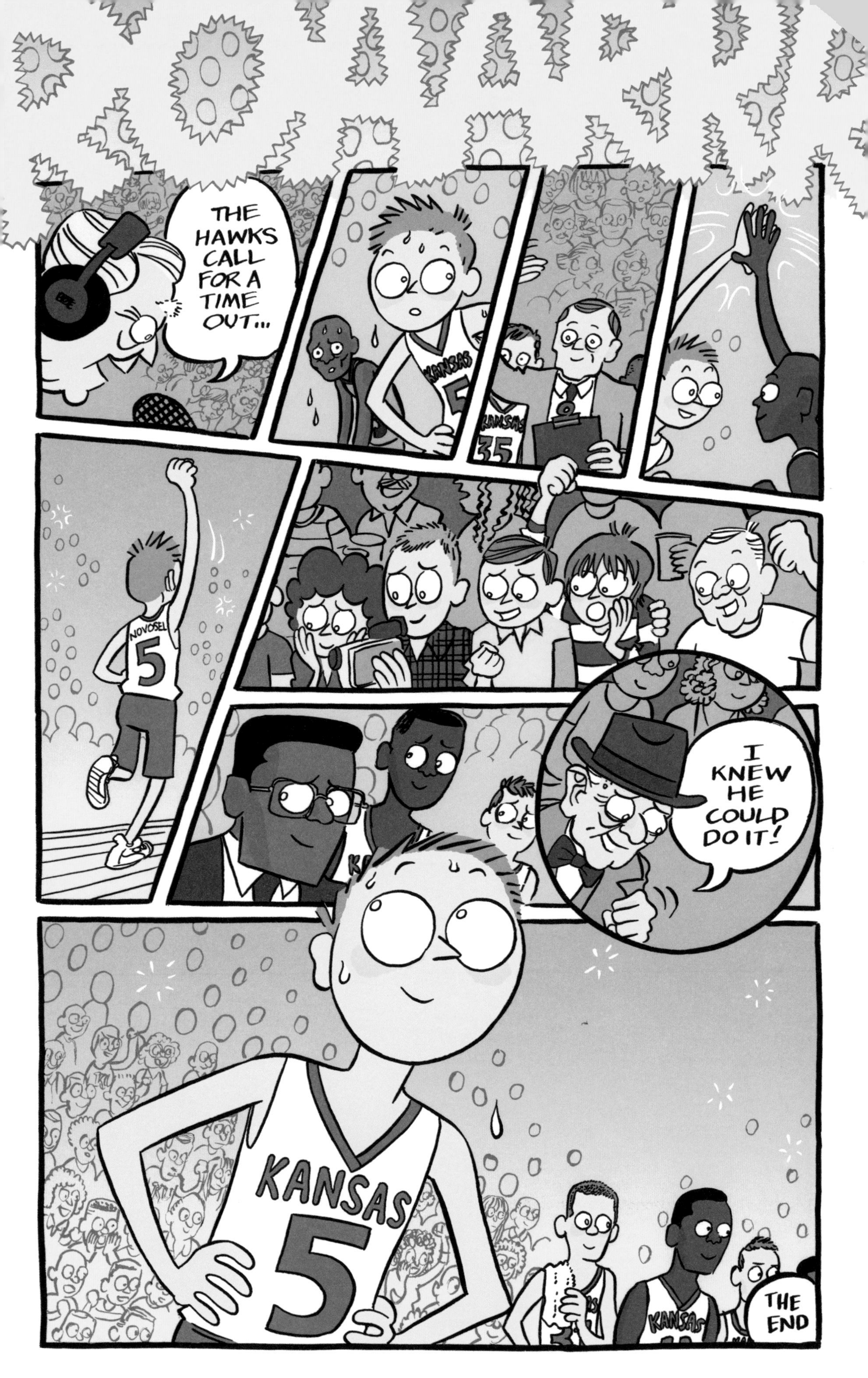
THE HAWKS CALL FOR A TIME OUT...
KANSAS 5
KANSAS 35
NOVOSEL 5
I KNEW HE COULD DO IT!
KANSAS 5
KANSAS
THE END

Notes:

Pg 4: "What you can conceive and believe, you can achieve." - Napoleon Hill

Pg 17: "To move a mountain, you must first begin by moving stones." - Confucius

Pg 60: "Things turn out best for the people who make the best of the way things turn out." - John Wooden

Fieldhouse is © 2015 Fieldhouse LLC

This is a first edition printed 2015.

All artwork and characters within © 2015 Scott Novosel Sam Sharpe and Fieldhouse LLC

All rights reserved no part of this publication may be reproduced or transmitted in any form or by any means, electronic or mechanical, including photocopying, recording or by any information and storage retrieval system, without prior written consent from the publisher.

Published by Fieldhouse LLC

Printed in USA

ISBN: 978-0-9768353-8-7